MW00344878

Level fields of play

Bobby Shows' life and ministry through sports

By James O. Preston, Jr.

Published by JOP Publishing
Jefferson City, Missouri

Images courtesy of Bobby Shows' personal files

First published 2013

Manufactured in the United States

ISBN 978-0-9894181-0-2

Notice: The information in this book is true and complete to the best of our knowledge. It is offered without guarantee on the part of the author or publisher. The author and publisher disclaim all liability in connection with the use of this book.

This book is dedicated to the memory of
Bobby's parents Carroll and Lucille Shows

CONTENTS

CHAPTER 1

Flight from Starkville

The call came in – time to move.

Since the night before, a cloud of uncertainty had hung over the usually upbeat road game routines of the Mississippi State University men's basketball team. "Are we playing or not?" they all wondered aloud and to themselves throughout the evening's preparations. Now, unleashed from their night-long ordeal, the tall young Mississippians sporting pressed slacks, jackets and narrow ties poured out of the dormitory onto the waiting van. Clean and spit-polished, with neat crew cuts perched atop scrubbed temples and shaved chins, the Bulldog varsity basketball team left campus just as though heading on any other road trip. But nothing much about this trip would be like any other. Led by assistant varsity coach Jerry Simmons, the varsity hurried to the Starkville airport. The date was March 14, 1963.

The previous day, two state legislators, staunch advocates of segregation, filed an injunction to keep the team from playing a game against a school with African-American players.

News of the injunction quickly reached Starkville. Its targets: University President Dean W. Colvard, Coach James "Babe" McCarthy, and Athletic Director Wade Walker. All three had anticipated the action against them and swiftly moved to get the team out of town.

To enforce the injunction, authorities had to serve papers to the defendants named in the writ. The basketball team itself was not included as defendants, which university officials had anticipated. Sensing law officers would leave the team alone and focus on serving papers to them, the three university officials quickly left town, but not before Coach McCarthy gave instructions for extracting the team from the deteriorating situation.

Some Starkville residents would later say the team escaped in the middle of the night, most likely confusing the team's departure with the odyssey of the university's president and the coach and athletic director who departed in different directions.

The players learned of the injunction as they settled into their usual routine the night before a road game. Doug Hutton, a junior guard, would remember that night: "We were sitting in somebody's dorm room when we heard about the injunction on the radio. We talked about jumping in our cars and taking off for Michigan. We were all anxious. We wanted to go. We wanted to play because we felt like we could compete with the best teams."[i]

Early the next morning, the unlikely foil in Coach McCarthy's scheme was team trainer Werner "Dutch" Luchsinger, who led the second team as a decoy to the airport in case the authorities tried to interfere. Meanwhile, the first team waited at the dormitory.

When Dutch and the faux team arrived at the airport, there were no authorities waiting to stop them. Now they ran into another snag – there was no plane. Thunderstorms delayed the flight scheduled to arrive at 8 a.m. To make matters worse, the deputy sheriff drove up to the team van as it sat idling on the tarmac. After a quick inspection, the deputy found no defendants. With no plane and no one on whom to serve papers, the officer left the airport, leaving "Dutch" and the second team in the van next to a hundred or so well-wishers who had come to see the team off.[ii]

Finally at nearly 9 a.m. a plane was on its way. Dutch telephoned Simmons to hustle the first team and top reserves to the airfield. The plane with the Bulldog contingent left Starkville at about 9:45 a.m.

The flight from Starkville to Nashville did not take long. Once on the ground, the team found Coach McCarthy and together they quickly boarded another plane bound for the first game of the Midwest Region of the 1963 National Collegiate Athletic Association tournament.

For the head coach and the team's senior players the journey to this point had been a long and sometimes frustrating pilgrimage. Wanting nothing more than to compete and prove they deserved a chance at a national title, finally, after three long years of battling, the Mississippi State University basketball team would get that chance.

Coach McCarthy's winning ways had already brought four Southeastern Conference (SEC) championships to Starkville in just eight years.[iii] There were the seniors from McCarthy's stellar recruiting class of 1959, starting with W. D. "Red" Stroud, the 6'1" floor general who led the Maroon charge all three championship years. Joining him as a three-year starter, athletic forward Leland Mitchell led the team in offensive production. Along with Mitchell and Stroud, stood 6' 5" strongman and team captain Joe Dan Gold. Rounding out the group of seniors was the man most highly regarded as a recruit in 1959 – post player Bobby Shows.

James O. Preston, Jr.

CHAPTER 2

Big Fish, Little Pond

Bobby Shows' early years in rural Mississippi during the 1940s and 1950s are almost storybook quality. Segregation was more than black and white; it was saved and lost. Mississippi buckles the Bible Belt synched down tight. Though humble, Bobby enjoyed a happy childhood, raised by two strong parents and surrounded by family, friends, and a faith community.

Outsized fits Bobby Shows.

When he smiles you wonder how a mouth could spread that wide with straight teeth in rows talking a language all their own. Then he speaks and the words betray his origins south – way south -- about as Deep South as you can get without a boat. Mississippi is long and narrow from north to south and most of Bobby's upbringing took place in southern Mississippi – places more backwoods and rural than urban, places where everybody says "yes ma'am" and "yes sir," places where the church sits prominently in the center of local geography and society, places a stone's throw from good fishing and a swimming hole, places a child can explore all day and most of the night without a parent worrying – a good place for a boy to grow up straight and true.

You can hear all that and more in Bobby's voice, not so much by what he says as how he says it.

When he reaches out to shake your hand, his long fingers seem to almost wrap twice around yours. At a shade under 6' 8", his size fits his personality. They call it charm. Coupled with natural good looks – tall, blue-eyed, athletic build – when he enters a room, everybody notices.

The hair has greyed, his gait slowed and his body stooped a bit with age, but there is still a twinkle in his eye. And when he talks about his passions -- Jesus Christ, wife Peggy Jane, and basketball – he is absolutely engaging.

Carroll and Lucille Shows' wedding day July 4, 1935.

Birthday

Long and not so lean at 10 pounds, 12 ounces, Bobby Shows entered this world large on October 10, 1941, the son of Robert Carroll and Lucille Shows. At the time, he was the largest baby born in Baptist Memorial Hospital in Jackson, Mississippi.

"Momma always kidded everybody that because of my length it took two days to get me through the birth canal," Bobby said. "She always made fun about how long I was. I was 24 inches long. That's two foot. That's a pretty good sized baby."

Bobby would say about growing up in the country that he was a big fish in a small pond. At his size, the pond couldn't be too small. Bobby's birth occurred just shy of two months from the infamous date December 7, 1941, and the bombing of Pearl Harbor. America, it was said at the time, was like a sleeping giant awakened from a long slumber. Mississippi and much of the South sent their young men and provided vital sea and air coastal defense during the war, following a long and venerated military tradition. Culturally, however, the South did not follow the quickened pace of change in America hastened by victory in a world war, but continued in its sleepy ways for a long time, well beyond the war years.

Family

If Mississippi were divided in thirds from north to south, the southern-most third would start about where Jackson lies and Interstate 20 crosses east and west the width of the state. Bobby's last name rhymes with "cows." The Shows family originated from rural Jones County in that southern-most part. At 6' 4," the Rev. James Knox Polk Shows, Bobby's great-grandfather, survived the Civil War even though he stood conspicuously almost a full foot taller than the average soldier. The Shows family has a picture of him sitting in a chair wearing his Confederate soldier's hat, with large hands poking out of his sleeves.

Scotty, Bobby's brother, described their father's parents as Christian people and subsistence farmers who raised nine children near Mozelle in Jones County. "They just never had anything. I can remember him talking about getting a piece of fruit for Christmas," Scotty said about his father.

The Shows' grandparents were like a majority of rural people in 1920s America. They had little education themselves. They worked hard and struggled to survive. At one point, Carroll Shows, Bobby's daddy, dropped out of high school. "He and his older brother decided they were going to get 40 acres and a mule and make a killing on crops. That was 1929, so you know what happened," Scotty said.

In a theme that would repeat itself throughout the Shows' family story, a coach intervened to help. At his former high school coach's urging, Carroll returned to school and eventually graduated from college where he played several sports, including football and basketball. Carroll could have ended up like his folks, struggling to make a living on a farm, but, as Scotty said, "Instead he chose to get educated and he coached about 20 years and then was an administrator for the next 20 years."

Lucille Berry, Bobby's mom, was raised on a truck farm between Georgetown and Pinola in Simpson County, Mississippi, with nine brothers and sisters. According to Scotty, their grandfather Berry, or "Papa B" as the grandchildren called him, had a truck farm where he raised tomatoes, cabbage, string beans, and a variety of vegetables to be sold wholesale to grocers. The Berrys were fairly well off, according to Scotty. His momma grew up living in a good-sized farm house that was not luxurious but was one of the nicer farmsteads in the area.

Both sets of grandparents had Christ in their home, according to Scotty, instilling faith and good character in the children, who passed those values to their children. Glenn Shows, Bobby's youngest brother, said that he and his brothers owe who they are and what they have accomplished to that faith legacy. He recalled a story about his mother's grandmother, a godly woman and prayer warrior. She died in 1941, the year Bobby was born. Glenn remembered hearing older aunts talk about how she prayed for a missionary, and all three of Lucille's children became ordained ministers and active missionaries all of their lives.

All three boys remembered their mom went to college on a bale of cotton. Lucille Berry attended Copiah-Lincoln Community College in Wesson, Mississippi. "Her daddy raised cotton and he would get momma into school and promise them a bale of cotton when pickin' time came," Bobby said.

At 5' 10" tall, Lucille played college basketball. According to Scotty, she is a member of her college's athletic hall of fame. While playing basketball for Copiah-Lincoln, Lucille jumped center in a game against the renowned female athlete, Mildred "Babe" Didrikson Zaharias. Zaharias won gold medals in track at the 1932 Olympics, gained All-American status playing college basketball, and was a championship professional golfer. Glenn remembers his mother saying the only thing she remembered about playing Zaharias was her kneecaps, "She would say, 'When I jumped center all I saw was her kneecaps.'"

Carroll Shows went to college on a football scholarship where at 6' 1" and 210 pounds, he played tackle. He attended Jones County Junior College in Ellisville, Mississippi. Both he and Lucille completed degrees at the University of Southern Mississippi in Hattiesburg. On July 4, 1935, Carroll and Lucille Shows united in marriage.

Maps of Mississippi show state and local highways spreading out in all directions from Jackson, the capital, like tentacles from a great jellyfish, including old U.S. 51, U.S. 49, and old U.S. 80 to name a few. The Shows family lived as itinerant educators in towns and villages scattered along those roads, places like Mount Olive and Mendenhall, Decatur and Hazlehurst, Union Church and Mars Hill, and finally Brookhaven.

Bobby adored his parents. "They were the best, most dedicated Christian parents that anybody could have," he said. "Daddy is my idol. Momma was the keeper of my soul. She always was more interested in what I was doing spiritually and livin'-wise." According to Bobby, his daddy took up coaching for the first time at Mount Olive, and eventually moved up U.S. Highway. 49 to Mendenhall, where they lived when Bobby was born.

The next move took the Shows family over what today is Interstate 20 to East Central Junior College in Decatur, Mississippi. Carroll coached football and basketball and served as a residence hall assistant, which allowed the young family to live in the dormitory.

Bobby was not in school yet, and his memories are limited to going to the football field and being with his daddy in the afternoons and on the basketball court in the evenings. "I remember one time I saw the boys taking those pills and I decided I'd like some so I took a handful and it was salt tablets and I got sick as a dog," he said.

Bobby followed his daddy around everywhere. Carroll took a strong interest in his son's physical well-being, allowing Bobby to work out with the football team and do pushups with the players. "Of course I was a little bitty kid, you know, 5'4" and five years old," Bobby said.

Hazlehurst

From Decatur, the family backtracked over Interstate 20 and down I-55 to Hazlehurst, where Bobby started school. While at Hazlehurst, the Shows family grew to include Scotty and later Glenn. Bobby would spend most of his elementary school years in Hazlehurst. "Daddy and momma made great decisions, but the only bad decision that I can remember they made was they started me to school when I was only five," Bobby said. "I turned six in October. You had to be six by October 1. But because I was such a big boy, the school agreed to

Bobby at four with his brother Scotty in Meridian, Mississippi

let me start before I turned six and I turned six ten days later. Which if I'd waited a whole other year, physically, I mean I know what I was like a year after I graduated from college and I played ball then. I'd a been another Bailey Howell!"

Growing up in a sleepy southern town like Hazlehurst provided fertile fields of fun for boys itching for something to do. Bobby recalls playing with his brothers on a big sand pile at an old construction site. "My brothers and I would build forts out of sand and we'd put sticks – we didn't have any soldiers so we had sticks for our soldiers – along the edge of the bank and we'd stand off and I'd throw a rock at his fort and he'd throw a rock at my fort. And we'd take turns and whoever had the last stick standing was the winner of the battle."

Bobby acquired a BB gun through a contest at the local drycleaner that gave a prize for collecting the most coat hangers. "You get coat hangers and tie 'em up by the fifties or the hundreds. And I happened to get the most so I got me a BB gun," he said.

Bobby and his BB gun quickly found mischief. A couple of other boys on his street had BB guns. Ammunition was cheap and easily accessible from any dimestore or farm supplier. For pennies a boy could purchase a tube of a thousand of the tiny steel projectiles. Armed and ready, the young bandits faced off across the street from each other.

Bobby recounted one such battle: "I remember one time the Renfro boy – I can't remember his first name – came over and he got pretty close and it got to stingin' when he hit me. So I went and got my gun and he stuck his head out and I caught him – right there (pointing to his temple) – he went home crying to daddy. And his daddy came over – and my daddy got involved and sent me upstairs. And I don't know what all took place downstairs but, uh, when he got through I do know what happened after that. I got a good tannin' for that one. No more BB gun fights after that."

Life centered on family and that meant extended family, too. Bobby said he remembers spending time with grandparents. He recalled his momma's daddy: "My daddy in the early days would go and help Papa B farm in the summertime and I would stay with Papa B most of the time and that's where I learned to plow with a mule." Bobby's memories of his daddy's folks were less pleasant. Carroll was one of ten children who split time keeping their aging parents. Carroll took his turn. Bobby's grandma had symptoms of dementia or Alzheimer's disease and his grandpa was crippled for most of his life. "Daddy said he farmed a lot but I never did see him farm," Bobby said.

Like many children in the South, Bobby had his first religious experiences early in life. Church was the spiritual center and the center of society in the small towns of southern Mississippi. Everyone attended Vacation Bible School and revival meetings, no matter his or her age or standing before God.

Southern Baptists are known for their evangelistic fervor. At regular intervals, the pastors of Baptist churches invite other pastors or professional evangelists to come and hold evangelistic meetings to make converts to the faith. The driving force behind these evangelistic efforts is Matthew 28:18-20, a passage known as the Great Commission, which calls on the faithful to evangelize, baptize new believers and bring them into the fellowship of the church.

The Shows family attended First Baptist Church of Hazlehurst. According to Bobby, First Baptist Church held such a meeting and he and his family attended. He said he was probably in the fifth grade.

These evangelistic meetings, or revivals as they were called, could last two or three weeks. As the preacher concluded this night's meeting, he invited people to get out of their seats and come to the front of the church for prayer to receive forgiveness of their sins and to have a personal relationship with Christ. Every Baptist Church worth its salt finished each service with a similar invitation, which is still true today.

One of Bobby's friends responded to the preacher's invitation and went down. "So I thought I'd go down, too," Bobby said. Having made their "profession" of faith, the preacher soon had Bobby and his friends in the baptistery pool. Bobby described being immersed: "We were dipped and dripped dried, you know, for God." Bobby was baptized at Hazlehurst Baptist Church on September 11, 1949, by the church's pastor, Rev. Rowe C. Holcomb.

At the time the experience was so exciting Bobby wanted to tell everyone. "I went home that day and the first thing this neighbor boy that I shot, he came over and I told him I was a Christian," Bobby said. "And I remember he said, 'What does that mean?' And I remember getting my Bible and I don't know what I said to him because I didn't know the Bible and I didn't know what had happened to me."

Bobby would get right with God when he was older. Yet some spiritual lessons stuck in spite of what Bobby described as a slow start. He recalled a visit to his cousin's house in New Hebron, south of Mendenhall on Route 43. The cousins went to the movies. Halfway through the show, the theater drew ticket numbers for a prize. "I remember they drew my number. And my cousin said it was his number. And we had a little scuffle back there and I got the number and I went down and they gave me five dollars," Bobby said.

Maybe it was out of guilt for scraping with his cousin. Or maybe he just wanted to do something good. When Bobby returned home, the boy's missionary education group at church called Royal Ambassadors, asked for money to give to missionaries. "For some reason or another, I gave them all five dollars of my money. I think that was my first real venture into missions," Bobby said.

Bobby recalled his time in Hazlehurst fondly, remembering a lot of firsts: his first bicycle, participating in Cub Scouts, playing Little League baseball and having his only experience playing football. But basketball was not part of his experience. Basketball would come later.

Union Church

As Bobby finished the fifth grade, his daddy took the family down State Route 28, southwest from Hazlehurst to Union Church, Mississippi, where Carroll became the principal and basketball coach. Union Church was a consolidated school and truly rural, little more than a crossroads with two stores, a church and the school. According to Bobby, at one time the school didn't have buses, so many of the students who lived far out in the country stayed in a dormitory throughout the week and only went home on the weekend. By the time the Shows arrived, the district had school buses and no longer boarded students. The old dormitory was converted to accommodate families who worked for the district. The Shows family lived in the dormitory, which they shared with three other families.

Bobby remembered the size of the building. "It probably would have – I know it housed four families at one time," he said. "And it probably could have handled six or eight – it had that many rooms in it." In the middle of the house was a large room, large enough for Carroll to assemble a makeshift ping pong table from a plywood board that lay across two sawhorses.

Bobby recalled they had a vegetable garden, a milk cow and hogs, but there were other critters, too, and not all were welcome. "I remember one time momma going out the steps and stepping on a rattlesnake. That was very exciting to hear her hollering and screaming!" Bobby exclaimed.

Two hoops stood sentry over a dirt court for basketball. The junior high and senior high building lay beyond the court. A little building held the elementary classes about 200 yards further away.

Three rooms held dual classrooms for first and second grade, third and fourth grade, and fifth and sixth grade. Bobby started there in the sixth grade. Recess and lunch provided opportunities to play baseball on a pasture next to the school. Bobby recalled those games often resulted in fights. Without an umpire and nothing but rocks for bases, Bobby said, "We did a lot of telling each other how to eat the cabbage."

While at Union Church, Bobby said, "Daddy 'let' me be the janitor. I cleaned up the big high school and the elementary school. I got $15 dollars a month, which was big time. After I got my first check, I bought my single 16-gauge shotgun. That was a big thing for me. We did a lot of squirrel hunting, rabbit hunting, and things like that." Bobby gave that shotgun to his oldest grandson, Cole, on his thirteenth birthday.

Rural people in the early 1950s didn't have money to spend on expensive sporting goods. Part of the fun was making your own equipment. Bobby described how one of the men whose family lived in the dormitory made his own fishing lures from chord and wax that they fished like a fly-rod.

Everyone living in the Mississippi countryside kept livestock. The Shows always had a sow and a litter of pigs. "We'd take one and feed it corn about two or three weeks. And then we'd kill it for our meat. And we'd sell the others. And put it (the money) back and then next year we'd 'bout do the same thing. And daddy always had a big garden. We probably had an acre garden, there, which always kept us out of trouble," Bobby said. Every morning Bobby milked the cow, sometimes two cows. He also fed the hogs. According to Bobby, his daddy got the food, or slop, for the hogs from the food trash at the school cafeteria. Bobby said he and Scotty had the job every afternoon of getting the slop two or three hundred yards up a hill on a gravel road without spilling it out of the little Flyer wagon outfitted with a zinc tub. In the afternoon, as janitor, Bobby had to clean the buildings until suppertime. After supper, he did homework, then to bed. "It was a pretty big routine," Bobby said. "During the school year, that took pretty much the whole day."

Saturdays the family sometimes went to town. Bobby said his parents would take the boys to Fayette or Hazlehurst for a movie and to get a haircut in the afternoon if they got all their jobs done in the morning. While he and his brothers watched the movie, Bobby said, "Momma and daddy would sit out on the front end of their car and talk to people. That was their form of recreation."

Sometimes the movies would come to a little country store between Pinola and Georgetown near where Bobby's grandpa lived, probably along what is today State Route 28. Bobby remembered watching old reel-to-reel movies in a tent set up outside. He and Scotty would pay their money and go inside. "There were old benches and they'd show a movie, usually an older black-and-white one," Bobby explained. "I remember Tarzan, the Lone Ranger. That's the two that come to mind. They were the 'el cheap-o's' where they'd ride the horses for half the movie and they kept going by the same rock. Every gun had 40 clips in it, you know, they'd just kept firing: POW! A lot of times we were about the only two white kids in there."

As a family, the Shows would sometimes go to the drive-in movie, once a fixture of many little towns across the south. They would drive to a roadside park for a picnic. "One particular roadside park featured an artesian well that provided our picnic beverage," Bobby said.

Other entertainment would come to the little village from time to time. Though the town was too small for a circus, Bobby said, "A bear wrestling guy would come around about once a year – brought this black bear. He was already full grown but he wasn't but about that high (Bobby gestured waist high) and if you could throw the bear you won a prize. I never did go into the ring with him but I watched some of the young strappin' 19- to 25-year-old men try to throw that bear. They had him muzzled and his claws clipped and I never did see anybody throw that bear. That bear would beat 'em up good."

Fishing and camping filled summer days and nights in Union Church. "We didn't have tents and stuff," Bobby said. "There was a big creek and we'd meet down there and bring our Vienna sausage and cheese and crackers, and we'd spend the night or whatever and fish on the creek banks."

Other forms of recreation included swimming in the swimming holes, various forms of combat with any available ammunition – corn cobs, rotten fruit, anything readily available for boys to pitch at each other. Sometimes the boys would test how far they could toss an object. Boys being boys, Bobby and his brothers sometimes chose cow patties for their challenge. "If we were real bold we'd throw some that were not quite dry," Bobby laughed.

According to Bobby, living in Union Church was fun. He recalled the man who ran the grocery store kept big tubs of ice cream for scooping cones and other confections. "When it would get down to where it was just the nibblins, he would call us – me and a couple of other boys – and we'd come down and we'd get into those barrels and finish up the ice cream," he said.

A Union Church boy knew he'd reached manhood when he could take a hundred-pound sack of feed, put it on his shoulder and put it in his pickup truck. "You'd become a man at that time and I remember I became a man about the 7th grade," Bobby said.

The Shows boys had to be confident in their manhood for another reason: their momma's tailoring. "Momma would take the feed sacks. Feed sacks used to have designs on 'em. Momma made all of our shirts out of that stuff. I still itch!" Bobby said, "The thing was, she didn't have a male pattern. It was all female. I don't know if you know but the female shirts button on the opposite side. And that was always the most confusing thing to button your shirt up, you know."

A lot of kids smoked cigarettes growing up, but Bobby never did. "I did smoke a lot of cross vines – that's a grapevine. I got whupped just as bad doing that as most kids would get smokin' cigarettes."

Bobby remembers playing a lot of baseball during their days in Union Church. Every Saturday the boys played community games, sort of like town teams coached by an adult. Any chance of Bobby becoming a pitcher was spoiled playing one afternoon on the Union Church field. Bobby said the team they were to play was tardy so the coach called a scrimmage and put Bobby on the mound. "I pitched nine innings. About the time I got through, this team showed up and I was the only pitcher. And I had to pitch another nine innings. After that I couldn't break a window pane if I had to. It ruined my arm. I could always throw junk but I couldn't throw anything probably more than fifty miles an hour," Bobby said.

Bobby and Scotty played a game called bunt ball. Two people could play bunt ball in limited space with only a ball and a bat. "We'd found an old bat that had been broken so we got some nails and tacks and tacked it together." As Bobby tells it, Scotty had a temper. During one game of bunt ball, Bobby said he got tickled about something Scotty did. Scotty didn't like it so he started flailing at Bobby. Bobby reached out and grabbed Scotty. "He broke loose from me, and as he was breakin' loose, I hit him with my elbow and that was when he got the bat. So I took off running," Bobby said. "As I was going through the screen door, he let that bat loose and it caught me right across the back and laid me colder than a cucumber right there on that floor. And momma was coming out the door about that time. Both of us – it wasn't fair, he should of gotten a whuppin –both of us got one more bad one." Bobby said Scotty's tooth was black for most of his life from Bobby's elbow. "It killed it. I would have been mad, too." Scotty remembers years later Bobby returning from college and asking him whatever happened to his temper and Scotty explained, "You left home!"

As the Shows family moved from place to place, if anyone bothered Scotty, he would tell them to leave him alone, that he had a big brother. "I wasn't kidding either – he was bigger than anyone else," he said. Scotty remembered the freedom of growing up in those small Mississippi hamlets. "We would ride our bicycles just anywhere in town, go to movies by ourselves and we were just 6 or 7 years old. Bobby was always the big brother, he was always the leader. He'd get us into trouble but he was always the one to get us out of trouble, too."

The school at Union Church burned during Bobby's seventh grade year. The weather turned cold sometime around Christmas. The buildings in the school complex were built of yellow pine, milled from the nearby forests and tree farms. Bobby recalls it burned hot, and in a matter of minutes, the building was gone. "The fear was that the big dorm we lived in was gonna catch on fire," Bobby said.

Besides the dirt basketball court and an area to play horseshoes and washers, there was not much room between the buildings. To protect the dormitory, they began hosing down the roof with water. But the wind was blowing so they decided to get everything out of the house. Bobby's mother was a stout person. She and another lady carried the piano from upstairs all the way down by themselves. "It took four men to get it back up. And how those two women got that done I'll never know, I'll never know," Bobby said.

Scotty said the survival of the living quarters was the first miracle he ever saw or heard about. "We'd got on our knees and prayed and asked God to change the direction of the wind." Later that year, Scotty walked the aisle at the end of a service at the little Union church in town and became a Christian, acknowledging, "That was when I was saved."

After the fire, the dormitory served as the schoolhouse, so the Shows and other families had to find someplace else to live. There wasn't much to choose from. The house the Shows chose didn't have indoor facilities or running water. "I don't even think it had a heater.

But I know we didn't have a bathroom and we had to draw water from a well on the back porch," Bobby said

Bobby played his first basketball game while at Union Church against a team from Hazlehurst. His father put the game together between teams made up of fifth- and sixth-grade boys.

Bobby remembered that most games were played outside and often on little more than a hard patch of ground next to a field, basketball hoops set opposite one another in an approximation of a court. On one such hard-scrabble court, Bobby said, "You tried to pick the uphill end of the court to start the game so you could finish it goin' downhill."

It didn't take long to see Bobby had a talent for basketball. He said he made the team and lettered as an eighth grader. By then, basketball captivated Bobby's attention. It became his god, he said, as he got more attention for his height and prowess on the court.

Bobby had plenty of other distractions to keep basketball from completely consuming him, though. Girls caught his eye by then. In that day, boys and girls related differently to one another. At parties they played a game called "Penny-go-walking." Girls sat opposite the boys in a line. One boy and one girl each received a penny. The boy went down the line of girls and dropped his penny in one of the girls' hands. And the girl went along the boy's side and dropped her penny into a boy's hand. The two who gave away their pennies, then left the group together. Meanwhile, the two who received got up and gave away their pennies before leaving together. The play is repeated until no one is left in the room. "Eventually there's nobody there unless they come back. Sometimes they did and sometimes they didn't," Bobby laughed.

Making the basketball team as an eighth-grader held some prestige but also had a downside, Bobby spent the season riding the bench. But he wasn't alone – he had a partner at the end of the bench – Sonny Gamble. Sonny and Bobby shared everything that year, splinters riding the bench, bruises providing practice for the first team, and girlfriends. It was Bobby's first girlfriend and a very innocent affair. "Between me and Sonny, I was her boyfriend today and tomorrow he was her boyfriend. And yet me and Sonny were the best of friends," Bobby said

Sonny and Bobby also shared a uniform – one uniform between the two of them. Union Church only had an outdoor dirt court so all games were played away from home. "Sonny had just come

Bobby practices his shot at about the age of twelve.

in from a game and he gave me the bag – little bag with the uniform in it," Bobby said. "For some reason or another I wasn't paying any attention about it to what was in there. So we went to Red Lick and went back to the dressing room for the next game. We were dressing and I was doing the same thing I normally do, but, there was no shorts in there. There was warm-up bottoms, warm-up top and the jersey, but no shorts."

As a practice player all year, Bobby believed he had little, if any, chance to get in the game, so he just pulled his warm-up bottoms over his jockey strap, put on the jersey and warm-up top, and headed for the bench. At some point late in the game, "While I was watching the spiders on the wall and that kinda stuff, so help me, Coach Johnson called me to come in the game. And not realizing what I had on or thought I had on, I ripped those-warm ups off and bent over," Bobby laughed.

A few years ago, Bobby, Jane and his two brothers went back to Union Church for a speaking engagement, and the church hosted a supper for them. "The first thing when I walked in, they all started laughin' and pointin'," Bobby said. "They didn't remember me for anything I had done since then except for that Red Lick incident of yankin' my pants down and showin' my hiney."

Black people

Mississippi in the mid-20th century was a magical place to grow up as a white boy, especially if you had athletic talent. Named for the "river that is beyond all age"[iv] that defines its western boundary, Mississippi is a land of forests and small farms, villages and towns. At best, most outside the south know little about the state, except for what they recall from a Faulkner novel or, more recently, a John Gresham story. At worst, outsiders have a picture of Mississippi clouded by attempts to repress civil rights activities in the 1950s and 1960s. Framed in black and white, white verses black, frozen in time and in the mind's eye, these events unfolded for the rest of the nation on television and in the newspapers.

Segregation was the law and the lay of the land. So thorough was the divide that Bobby admits he knew little about the black community in the places they lived. When Glenn, his youngest brother, was little, there was an old black couple that came to live in a dilapidated shotgun house at Union Church down by the cow barn. The woman helped with Glenn while the old man did odd jobs around the farm for rent. "They must have been -- I mean, back then, they had to be 90 years old, you know -- they were probably 60 but they looked ancient to me," Bobby said.

The old woman cared for Glenn while his mother taught school. The couple didn't have a family of their own. The woman helped prepare food in the evenings. A coon hunter, the old man, according to Bobby, did "all kinda huntin' just so they could have something to eat, you know. We did try to get 'em some food out of the cafeteria. Daddy did. So they were fed. They didn't receive a salary, just had a place to live and the food. I got a picture of Glenn, of her holding him. That's the only picture we have of them that I know of," Bobby said.

"I don't know where the black kids went to school. I have no earthly idea. I've asked people where did they go to school. I know where they went in Hazlehurst, but in Union Church and Mars Hill, nobody [seemed to know] where they went to school, or if they went to school. I have no idea."

Bobby's lack of understanding was not exceptional. Most white people in southern Mississippi in the 1940s and 1950s were ignorant about the life of their African-American neighbors, so thoroughly was segregation engrained into the fabric of society. Bobby said the only time he might have seen a black person was when they would come to one of the two stores at Union Church. "I don't even know where they lived. When I was a little older we would play with black kids from time to time. They were just another opponent, another opportunity to compete with a basketball or baseball or whatever the sport."

Sports weren't the only thing common to the separate and distinct black and white communities. All knew "King Cotton" – a livelihood for many in the black community. For a white boy growing up in southern Mississippi, cotton provided a way to make a little extra money. Bobby recounted how, at both Union Church and Mars Hill, school didn't start until the first of October because of the cotton harvest. At Union Church "that was how we made our extra money was pickin' cotton, two cents a pound," he recalled. "And every afternoon after school, when I wasn't doin' something else or in particular on Saturdays, that's where we earned our cotton money."

To the cotton fields he would go to pick cotton alongside other boys like him, old black men and women and young ones, too. It didn't matter – under the scorching sun, the back-aching, finger-splitting work of picking cotton takes place on level fields. "We was pickin' one day and this little black girl – she couldn't have been any much older than what I was – and she was very heavy pregnant," Bobby recalled. "At lunch time she didn't come back. In a few minutes we heard this cry – little girl had that baby out there underneath a tree. One of them mid-wives had come and helped her have it. She had the baby and before the afternoon was over she was back pickin' cotton. Man alive, I mean she couldn't have been more than 13 or 14 years old."

By the time he entered ninth grade, Bobby was six feet tall and still growing.

Level Fields of Play

CHAPTER 3

An Unwritten Law

For eight years, Mississippi forbade teams from playing integrated games after a tournament in 1956 in which the Mississippi State men's basketball team played a game verses an integrated team. That game ultimately set up a showdown in 1963 between the State of Mississippi and the Mississippi State Bulldogs who won the SEC's automatic bid to the NCAA tournament for the third year in a row.

Any illusion of integration and equality did not extend beyond the cotton fields Bobby worked as a boy. "Separate but equal" may have been the slogan of segregation, but separation of the races remained the singular emphasis in the South. Equality was at best a secondary consideration.

But America was changing and the South was no exception. Many citizens of southern states recognized apartheid policies of the past were unsustainable and immoral. Yet, some in the South resisted change. The segregationists still wielded political clout in statehouses and county seats across the South.

The term "Jim Crow" refers to the laws and customs that sprang up after reconstruction in the 19th century to enforce segregation of the races.[v] By the middle of the 20th century, federal laws and court actions began to move against entrenched Jim Crow policies, enforcing change at the state and local level. Public schools and colleges served as the battleground, the place where new laws were tested and segregationists resisted.

Losing the battle in the classroom,[vi] segregationists shifted the fight to athletic playing fields and courts. Seeing opportunity in public-school athletics, legislators, universities, school boards, and officials of all kinds targeted basketball and other sports to extend segregationist policies.[vii]

As long as competition remained at the regional level, these policies went unchallenged and little noticed. Success of college teams across the South, however, forced the issue to the forefront, especially in football and basketball. Conference champions received bids to play in national bowls and tournaments in which they might face integrated teams. Under the unwritten law, teams could accept offers to participate against other segregated teams if the option existed, but had to bow out of invitations to play integrated teams.

Until the mid-50s, Jim Crow policies went virtually unchallenged in Mississippi. The unwritten law was no exception. Mississippi only occasionally enjoyed more than regional success in athletics. So when the football team at Jones County Junior College in Ellisville, played against an integrated team in the 1955 Junior Rose Bowl, a contingent of Mississippi legislators threatened to withhold future appropriations from any schools that did not refuse invitations to play integrated teams.[viii]

The legislature enacted no bill, nor did university boards establish any policy, but the efficacy of the unwritten rule was proven the very next year. In 1956, Mississippi State University in Starkville yielded to the policy after winning a first-round basketball game against an integrated team in a holiday tournament. Rather than allow the team to play a second game against another integrated team, Mississippi State University President Ben Hilbun ordered the squad to return home.[ix]

For eight years, Mississippi successfully enforced the unwritten policy preventing its teams from playing integrated games beginning in 1956 when Mississippi State acquiesced. As the Bulldogs piled up tournament wins and conference championships, the stakes ratcheted higher and higher, setting up a showdown with the segregationists in 1963 when Mississippi State University received the Southeastern Conference automatic bid to the NCAA tournament for the third year in a row.

James O. Preston, Jr.

CHAPTER 4

Basketball Will Be My Sport

Bobby played baseball and basketball growing up, but excelled at basketball from the eighth grade on, leading to an invitation to join the Mississippi State Bulldog Men's Basketball team in the fall of 1959.

Hundreds of crossroads intersect the Magnolia State.

Every village had a church, a school and a store. During the early 1950s, Mississippi began consolidating larger school districts with smaller, rural districts. Villages all over Mississippi saw their little schools go away and their kids bused to other towns. Union Church, where Carroll and Lucille worked, lost its school that year, consolidating into the Fayette school district. The year was 1955 and the Shows family moved once again. Bobby would start his freshman year at a new school in Mars Hill, in Amite County. Carroll became the superintendent at Mars Hill and taught American history and civics. Lucille taught second grade.

Mars Hill

The school building had two wings, one for the elementary school through the eighth grade and the other for the high school. Bobby remembered the Mars Hill School as very small. "When we left there I was the tenth member of the class. Only nine graduated out of my class. There were only 200 kids – that's how small it was."

Mars Hill had a church, a store and a school strung along the highway, and little else. Located where North Greenburg Road crosses County Road 570, the village sat about a mile from the west fork of the river from which the county took its name. The road through town was gravel when Bobby moved there.

Life for the Shows family continued to center on church, school and work. The family raised some of their own meat and supplemented table fare with the vegetables they grew. The boys did more hay hauling than cotton picking in Mars Hill.

"Daddy hired us out. God rest his soul. He would get the money for what we got and then he would give us a little bit. We were subsidizing the family income. Everybody that had hay wanted me because I was tall and I could throw (the bales) up on the wagon farther than some of the rest of them could so I had a busy job all the time," Bobby said.

The Shows' house was next to the school and across the street from Mars Hill Baptist Church. It had two bedrooms, a kitchen, a dining room, back porch, sitting area and was very small. "The three of us boys slept in one room. Scotty and I slept in a normal bed together," Bobby said. By then he was six feet tall. From the second grade to the eighth grade, Scotty's nickname was "Chubby." The two big boys managed to share the same small space, even if reluctantly. "We did not touch. There was an imaginary line down the middle of that bed and if you moved over in the middle of the night you got kicked!" Bobby laughed.

Scotty said he was tongue-tied as a boy. "I couldn't say my name. I'd say my name was 'Shoddy Shows,' and they'd say 'Shawdy' what? And Bobby, of course, would not help me. He'd sit there like he didn't know who I was so I'd have to spell my name out." At Mars Hill Bobby fashioned an escape of sorts from the close quarters he and Scotty shared by making a single-sized seven-foot-long bed in his mechanical arts class at school.

Life as the superintendent's son with both parents teaching pushed Bobby in school and taught him other lessons, not all of which he welcomed. Bobby remembers taking one of his father's classes. "He knew when I'd studied and when I didn't study. And I don't know what he was trying to prove but the nights I didn't study – guess what would happen – we'd have a pop test the next day. Some of the smart kids began to realize what was happening and I got verbally chastised for that so I had to study," Bobby said.

Sensibilities have changed since Bobby was in school, and the policies governing discipline have changed, too. But in the 1940s and '50s, public schools all across the United States not only allowed corporal punishment, it was encouraged as a pedagogical tool for training and maintaining discipline. Bobby experienced his share of learning from the business end of a paddle both in school and at home.

As a freshman, Bobby looked up to the seniors. One senior was a cousin who included Bobby in his social circle. Sometime during that year, the seniors decided they didn't like the food served in the cafeteria, that the menu was too dependent upon government-surplus commodities. "They decided they were going to get that changed. So they got a petition up and they asked me to sign something," Bobby explained. He was among the first people to sign so his name appeared near the top of the list. When Superintendent Shows got hold of it, he figured the people who had signed first were probably the instigators.

He called about a dozen people from among the top group of signatories to his office, with Bobby among them. Apparently, Superintendent Shows said little. "We was all bent over. He had the paddle and he was – when daddy got mad, he would bite his tongue – and I mean he was swinging for the fences." Superintendent Shows' judgment came swift and furious. For the seniors, at least, it passed quickly and then was over. But Bobby still had to go home. "I got home that day and – this is kind of humorous – but I can remember it just like it were yesterday.

"Daddy said: 'Bobby, I understand you got a spankin' today.'

"'Yes, Daddy, I got a spankin' today and I think I know who gave it to me.'

"'Well, the kids that got spankin's today I know what's happening to them tonight and guess what – you get one just like them because it's the same principle. Bend over.'

"And he wore me out again," Bobby laughed.

Bobby approached education like most kids, with ambivalence about school work, biding time until the final bell rang and he could head to practice. Though sports dominated Bobby's priorities, he still found time to participate in class plays and other activities. The practical arts captured Bobby's attention in high school. He became part of the hog judging team and learned to raise hogs and plant pine trees. In woodshop, Bobby made a cedar chest that he still has. He still has the seven-foot single bed he made in shop, too.

Outside of school Bobby tried his hand in an entrepreneurial venture. He and friend Jimmy Carruth built picnic tables. Bobby said a lumberyard gave them slab wood, scraps of rough wood leftover from the milling process. One side of the board was flat so Bobby and Jimmy turned the flat side up, slab side down, and constructed picnic tables that they sold for five dollars each. Eventually the lumber yard found out what they were doing and started charging them for the slab wood. "That cut out our profit pretty quick," Bobby said.

The Shows wasted no time getting involved in the church at Mars Hill as they had done at Union Church and every other place they lived. Carroll served as a Sunday School teacher and a deacon. Bobby joined the Royal Ambassadors, continuing his unbroken record of involvement from first grade until the end of his junior year. The church's pastor led the Royal Ambassadors program. He took the boys to other towns to play whatever sport was in season against other Royal Ambassador groups, rotating between communities. Bobby said the sports program attracted a lot of boys.

The Mars Hill church had an active program for youth. Bobby remembered a lot of church parties, "taffy pulls, peanut boilin's, watermelon cuttin's, things like that. Almost every Sunday night, one of the young people's parents would have us over, and we had a pretty big youth group. I'd say we had 20 or 25."

Growing up in the rural South, a young man learned how to shoot a gun and how to hunt. The boys did a lot of squirrel hunting and Bobby learned to hunt deer. "Daddy became a member of a deer club up around Port Gibson and Nachez so I went huntin' with him a lot. Back then you didn't use rifles. You used shotguns because you didn't go up in a tree, you stayed on the ground. Your stand was along a road – a loggin' road or something like that."

The Bostic Motor Company of McComb, the big town near Mars Hill, sponsored a baseball team during the summer. Bobby described his experience playing for the Bostic Motor Company team:

"I was a catcher – a 6'6" catcher. I was so slow coming out of a crouch because it just took me a long time to get out of it. They taught me how to drop to my knees and throw from my knees and I got pretty good throwing from my knees – made the All-Star team – I was real proud of that. I really wasn't a good baseball player at all. Nobody taught me how to bat. It was just you grab a stick and just swing."

During several summer breaks, the Shows family lived on the Southern Mississippi University campus while Bobby's parents continued their educations. "Daddy had five master's degrees," Bobby said. "They'd put us boys in the demonstration school. That gave us permission to use any of the facilities at Southern. So we could go to the pool; we could go down to the gymnasium to play basketball."

Bobby's focus on basketball grew with his stature, standing six feet tall by his freshman year. He would reach 6' 4" by his sophomore year. Not finished growing, he added two more inches his junior year and one more after that, reaching 6'7" by his senior year in high school. Basketball was king at Mars Hill. School didn't start until October, and games started as soon as school started. Bobby played enough his freshman year to earn a letter. He had lettered the previous year at Union Church. By the time his high school career ended, he had earned five letters in basketball and two in baseball.

Today, state high school athletic associations have policies limiting the number of games a team can play in a season, in a week, or even in a day. While he doesn't remember how many games were played other years, Bobby knows his team played more than 70 basketball games his junior year at Mars Hill. To put that number in perspective, today's National Basketball Association professional teams play an 82-game regular season. "I can remember going to some tournaments and maybe play three games in one day and turn around the next day and play two or three games, according to whether you won or lost."

Pavement was the exception and roads with shoulders were few on the ancient highways. Roads crisscrossing Mississippi made travel hazardous at times. Automobiles then lacked the standard safety features of today's cars. Accidents maimed and killed many people. A minor two-car accident or a one-car mishap might alter or end the occupants' lives. In spite of the risks, people fearlessly took to the roads. Some jobs – coaching was one – required automobile travel, regardless of the hazards. During one of those road trips, Bobby's sophomore year, his coach nearly lost his life and his driver, Bobby's daddy, Carroll Shows, nearly died.

Superintendent Shows had driven Coach Stewart to Brookhaven to help establish the seeding for the south regional basketball tournament. "On the way back they were hit head on by two guys racing. That was one of the tough experiences of my life," Bobby said. When the highway patrol investigated the scene, they discovered that Carroll had swerved six feet from the center line in an attempt to avoid the collision. As Bobby remembers it, emergency responders got Coach Stewart out but "didn't fool with daddy at all because they didn't think he would live anyway." Once they got Coach Stewart free, they returned to discover Carroll was still alive. The crash completely crushed his left side – his hip, knees, arm, ribs, the whole left side. They transported Carroll and Coach Stewart to the hospital in Brookhaven. As soon as the family learned of the accident, Bobby's momma, Lucille, went to the hospital. But Bobby had to stay with his two brothers.

Bobby learned later the doctors were so convinced Carroll would not make it that they didn't set his broken bones. They just kept him comfortable. Bobby doesn't remember how long his daddy lay there like that. After almost a week, Bobby still hadn't seen him. "Grady Burris, who was the chairman of the school board of education there, came by one night and said that he was going up to see daddy and would I like to go. His wife, 'Miss' Nela Ray, would stay with the boys." Finally, Bobby went to Brookhaven to see his daddy. For nearly a week, Carroll lay in a hospital bed barely moving, never opening his eyes, and not responding to anything. "When I walked into the room, he opened his eyes and spoke for the first time. He said, 'Bobby, you got to sell the hogs,'"

Everyone told Bobby later that he turned white as a sheet. Not only was he shocked to see his daddy in such bad shape, Bobby had never done more than slop hogs. He didn't know the first thing about selling them. The responsibility was quite different and seemed a little overwhelming. Mr. Burris stepped in to help, coming by the house a day or two later. "He helped load up the hogs and carry them to the auction where we sold them all," Bobby said. That was his first time to ever hear an auctioneer.

The accident happened late in basketball season sometime in March, and by summer Carroll was still recuperating. Bobby said they sent his daddy to the hospital in Jackson to reset all his broken bones. He was hospitalized for weeks, and came home in a wheelchair. Bobby learned a lot about his dad that summer.

"I was pitching baseball in a summer program and daddy said, 'Bobby, I'll catch you as long as you throw it to me because I'm not gonna get up out of this chair.' And he was in a wheelchair. And so he actually caught me day after day when I was working on my pitchin'. I probably learned more about the important things of life during those pitching engagements than I ever did anything else because he had my attention."

Carroll worked hard to come back from the accident. He followed a regimen of physical therapy to get his arm and shoulder back in shape. But his hip never fully recovered, and within a couple of years, Bobby said, big, strong, college athlete and former coach R. C. Shows couldn't walk on his own.

"That was a traumatic experience to go through my sophomore year. Coach Stewart eventually died in the middle of my junior year, mainly from the results of that wreck. He died and is buried there at Mars Hill. And daddy took over as the coach during my junior year and he coached me for probably three weeks, four weeks maybe, and took us to state," Bobby said. Mars Hill would place third at state that year, a feat that only one other team from Mars Hill would accomplish.

By his junior year, sportswriters had pegged Bobby as a major college recruit. Schools like Louisiana State and the University of Texas showed interest but Mississippi State seemed to have the early inside track. "Shows, a senior next year, already is getting 'feelers,' and rightly so, because State's Babe McCarthy knows where the talent is," said Jim Sellers, assistant sports editor for the Jackson *State Times*. "Show's father who is superintendent of Mars Hill High School, and a former East Central Junior College athletic director and coach at Meridian, says, however, that his boy ain't to be fooled with yet since he is only a junior."[x] Bobby led his Mars Hill team to a third place finish in the B-BB division that season.

School consolidation interrupted the Shows family once again, this time at the end of Bobby's junior year in high school. "I didn't want that to happen because I was fixin' to move to another place my senior year," Bobby said. By the time he and his family reached Brookhaven, Mississippi, Bobby was already established as a major college basketball prospect. Sports writers, coaches and basketball fans across the state knew the name Bobby Shows.

In Starkville, another 6' 7," 215-pound basketball player was capturing the imagination of the Magnolia State. Mississippi State was barely on the map of college basketball before Coach McCarthy arrived in Starkville. He recruited talented Bailey Howell from little Middleton, Tennessee, to come play for him in 1956, and by Howell's senior year, 1959, they had won the Southeastern Conference (SEC) Championship. Howell ranked in the top ten nationally three years running in scoring and rebounding. His double-double average has never been matched in the SEC, with 27.1 points and 17 rebounds per game at State. After his stellar college career, he took his game to the NBA where he played a dozen years, became an All-Star, won an NBA championship, and made the Hall of Fame.[xi]

Imagine, a kid from a little nowhere town doing all that. When Howell was a senior at State, Bobby was a senior at Brookhaven High School. While leading his team deep into the post-season, Bobby averaged 23 points a game. With a frame similar to Howell's, more than one observer would make the comparison: Would Bobby be the next Howell?

Bobby drives the lane for Brookhaven High School at the Mississippi State A-AA finals in 1959.

Brookhaven

Brookhaven suited Bobby. The new school was large enough but not too large for Bobby to have some experiences he might not have had otherwise. Bobby played trumpet in the band. He played high school baseball, and escorted the homecoming queen. He was voted "Most Friendly." After only attending one year at the school, Bobby was elected to the Brookhaven Hall of Fame.

Jim Sinclair coached the Brookhaven High School basketball squad and had a tremendous influence on Bobby's life.

"We were winning all our ballgames, but one night we just played well enough to win. We should have beat the team by twenty or thirty or more points and we ended up only winning by eight or ten. So the next day at practice coach wasn't very happy with us so he worked us pretty hard, in fact very hard. At the end of practice, I started to go in and he reached and grabbed me.

"He was about 6' 4" and we got nose to nose. He said, 'Bobby, did you play the best you could last night with the abilities that you have?' Of course, you could talk to me and I'd just melt. Daddy would have never had to whip me if he hadn't wanted to. (Coach Sinclair) was that kind of influence on me. He and his wife were over at our house every week to ten days. Daddy and him became very, very close friends."

Bobby described the team that year as loaded with talent, with the top six players all getting college athletic scholarships. Along with Bobby, the Edmonds twins got scholarships to play major college basketball. They played against Bobby at Ole Miss. Another teammate got a baseball scholarship to Mississippi College, and two more teammates got scholarships to junior college.

Ben McKibbens met Bobby a couple of years later in North Carolina where they both served as summer camp counselors, but he remembers seeing Bobby for the first time playing in the state tournament. McKibbens was a freshman football player at Mississippi College in Clinton. He and some others came to Jackson to watch Bobby and the Brookhaven team play. "I could not believe how good that team was and I can visualize now not just him, but all five of those starters. It was amazing how good a high school team they were. And Bobby was just so dominating," McKibbens said.

By the end of Bobby's senior-year campaign, the accolades flowed, including All-State honors and a nomination for All-American. Jimmy McDowell, sports editor for the Jackson *State Times* reported on the crowd of recruiters that showed up for the South Division Big Eight tournament in Hattiesburg. McDowell noted:

"College scouts sweetened the crowd: Ray Poole of Ole Miss., Dick Innman of Georgia Tech, Bill Dooley and Bobby Collins of State, the entire Mississippi Southern crowd, headed by athletic director Reed Green . . . All hands watching potential college prospects and certainly six-foot seven and a quarter-inch Bobby Shows . . . Papa Carroll watched with pride, saying that his boy would do nothing until the season had ended. Fred Lewis of Southern ardently courting Shows and his dad, who was a Mississippi Southern grad . . . 'That boy could play for us next year,' Fred said enthusiastically . . . 'Boy, could we use him! . . . And who couldn't?'"[xii]

By the end of March 1959, the Brookhaven Panthers had racked up 41 wins to only two losses, and just missed a state championship. Bobby's teammates commemorated his contribution by electing him permanent captain.[xiii] Bobby would end an honor-filled high school career at the top of Mississippi high school basketball. Considered the top prospect in the state, Bobby now had to take his game to the next level and choose a college.

Letter of intent

Sunday at the Shows' household meant church and family time and, occasionally, the company of friends and neighbors. On Sunday, March 15, 1959, the Shows family returned home after a morning in church, bringing a guest who had attended services that day – Coach Babe McCarthy, the young, dynamic head coach of the Mississippi State University Bulldog men's basketball team.

That afternoon, a meal was shared and a covenant struck between coach and parents. Coach McCarthy said that if Carroll and Lucille would entrust their son to him, he would take care of Bobby, help him get a college degree, and make him a college basketball player. In a double irony, Shows signed his college letter of intent exactly four years earlier to the day that his future team would finally get to play in the NCAA tournament. On the day Bobby signed his letter of intent, McCarthy would have been in Evanston, Illinois for the Mid-East Regional of the tournament rather than on the recruiting trail, had he been allowed to take the Maroons to the 1959 NCAA tournament as the SEC representatives.

Jimmy McDowell, sports editor for the Jackson *State Times*, would write about the events that day, reminding readers that the two-time, all-stater was a "huge youngster, who wears a size 15 shoe and possesses a tremendously large pair of hands." McDowell said Bobby was regarded the "number one prep hoop prospect in the Magnolia State," being pursued by Ole Miss, Mississippi State and Southern Mississippi. McDowell described McCarthy as "jubilant" about signing Shows.

"Shows was considered our top prospect. He is the big man that we had to have to make our program go and we're naturally very happy of his decision to join us at Mississippi State. Bobby might even grow to be six nine. He's not only a great player, but he's a fine boy, too," McCarthy said.

Bobby's father told McDowell: "Bobby made up his mind Sunday morning. The wife and I were surprised. We didn't think that he would decide so soon. Most of all we wanted the final choice to be his. After all, he is the one who must be happy."[xiv]

There in the living room of the Shows' home, Bobby signed a commitment to play basketball for Mississippi State University. McCarthy would fulfill his part of the covenant with Bobby's parents. Bobby, in turn, would do his part. Over the next four-plus years, Bobby would graduate with bachelor's and master's degrees, and learn how to be a college basketball player. More importantly, he would learn lessons that shaped the trajectory of his life and calling for years to come.

Jerry Clower was a friend of the Shows family and Bobby's Sunday School teacher part of his senior year at Brookhaven. Clower would one day carve out his own infamy as a country comedian with guest spots on the Grand Ole' Opry and the Hee Haw television program. But when Bobby was in high school, Clower was still a seed salesman who was just starting to gain popular recognition. Being a Mississippi State graduate, Clower started twisting Bobby's arm to commit to State. "He was always jabbing me about going to Mississippi State and not be one of those Rebels from over there," Bobby said, referring to State's rival, Ole Miss. Bobby recalled an encounter with Clower after signing with the Maroons. "After I signed he came to me and said, 'Now Bobby, this is legal, now that you've already signed and you are going to State, I want you to go down to the men's store and buy you a white sport coat.' I went down and I had to order it. Of course, they didn't have anything that fit me. And he bought me a linen white sport coat. That was when that song 'White Sport Coat' came out by Marty Robbins," Bobby said."[xv]

Bobby signs his letter of intent to play at Mississippi State for Coach James "Babe" McCarthy, March 15, 1959. Standing behind Bobby are his parents.

James O. Preston, Jr.

CHAPTER 5

A Special Coach

Babe McCarthy turned Mississippi State into a powerhouse basketball program and his 1963 team was led by a group of seniors who came to State with the expectation that they would do something special.

The round ballers pressed in around their infamous coach. One asked, "How do you win these games?"

Looking his sweating devotees square in the face, the coach said, "Boys, we win games one trip down the court at a time. When we play defense, it's going to be the best one. When we get the ball and we head to the other end of the court, it's going to be the best offensive showin' we've ever done. And we are just goin' to win 'em one at a time."

That, according to Bobby Shows, summed up the heart of the man who would lead Mississippi State to league and national prominence. "Babe McCarthy was one wonderful person," Bobby said. "And when he told us to jump, we said, 'How high?' We were just kids. We obeyed our coaches. So when Babe said about winning another SEC championship, 'Boys, if we win it again, we're going to play in that tournament, come hell or high water!' we believed him."[xvi]

Stubborn determination and a knack for sales made James "Babe" McCarthy great. Whether he was selling insurance, selling his players on their ability to win any game, or selling a state on sending his team north against the wishes of authorities, grit and a winning grin were as much behind his success as his mastery of game strategy. Bobby said McCarthy was a great psychologist with his players. He knew that running the stands got through to one player, when the next player might need a lecture. "Me, it wouldn't have done much good runnin' some hills, but to sit me down and talk to me like that – oh 'gawd' – I'd rather take a bull whippin' than I'd had that."

Aubrey Nichols, a guard on the team and one of Bobby's roommates in college, said the way McCarthy developed special relationships with his players allowed him to do just that. "I think every one of us to a man felt like we had a special relationship with our coach. For that reason you played hard for him. It was more than just a coach-to-player relationship; it was a person-to-person relationship."

McCarthy's sojourn to the helm of the Mississippi State Bulldog men's basketball team was an unlikely journey. He got a degree from State but never played college sports. He flew airplanes in World War II and coached a service basketball team to a division championship. When he returned to Mississippi, he took up teaching and coaching junior high and high school teams and was successful enough to gain a reputation as a great coach. But with a family to feed, McCarthy turned to a sales career.

When Mississippi State's athletic director sought to revive the men's basketball program in 1955, he gave McCarthy a call. Little is known about how McCarthy was chosen other than the athletic director trusted a recommendation to give McCarthy a shot. Bobby recalled McCarthy coached just ten years in Starkville and still holds the mark for highest winning percentage of any Mississippi State basketball coach. McCarthy would win four SEC championships during his tenure at State. He also was named collegiate Coach of the Year four times. He was admitted into the Mississippi Sports Hall of Fame in 1975.[xvii]

Bobby remembered McCarthy as a show man. During one game, McCarthy got very upset with the referees. "So he ran out into the middle of the court. And the referee says, 'Coach, for every step it takes you to get back to that bench I'm going to charge you a technical foul,'" Bobby said. "McCarthy stopped in his tracks, turned to the bench and said, 'Boys, come out here.' And three or four players bolted to McCarthy, picking him up and hoisted him to the bench. That referee just died laughing and forgot about the whole thing. He was that kind of guy."

In his ten years leading the Mississippi State University basketball team, McCarthy compiled a record of 169-85 for a winning percentage of .665 and won four SEC titles in a five-year span.

When he left MSU, McCarthy coached in the old American Basketball Association (ABA) for the Kentucky Colonels and teams in Memphis, Dallas, and New Orleans. He was named ABA Coach of the Year in 1969 and was honored as Co-Coach of the year in 1974. He was the first ABA coach to win 200 basketball games. McCarthy developed colon cancer in his last year with the Colonels and died in his hometown of Baldwyn, Mississippi, in 1975. He was 51 years old.[xviii]

Coach McCarthy poses with his sensational sophomores in 1960.

James O. Preston, Jr.

CHAPTER 6

A Roller Coaster Ride

Bobby's basketball career at Mississippi State, like that of most athletes, had its ups and downs. Bobby started for his undefeated freshman team, but the sophomore jinx bit him hard. After dedicating his life to Christ, Bobby returned with new focus for a stellar junior year.

Starkville in 1959 was small with a population of about 9,000.

But to Bobby, coming from rural Mississippi, it might as well have been a metropolis – off the beaten path, "You have to be coming here to go here, you don't just drop by," said one former Bulldog coach. To find Starkville, go 66 miles south from Elvis Presley's birthplace in Tupelo, or 128 miles north from Jackson.[xix]

Bobby said his freshman year he "kind of went from a big fish in a little pond to a little fish in a big pond."

If Bobby struggled in his transition to college, the move to the next level on the basketball court went better. NCAA rules barred athletes from playing varsity the first year. Teamed with arguably the best class of McCarthy recruits in the young coach's career, Bobby and his freshmen teammates posted an undefeated record and a sizzling 99.5 points per game scoring average, holding their opponents to 59.5 points per contest.[xx]

Coach McCarthy praised his 1959-1960 freshmen team for their efforts on the court. "They're even better than the fine team we had when Bailey Howell was a freshman," he said. "We don't have anyone in the class of Howell, who was a true All-American, but the team's balance is wonderful. We have seven kids who play most of each game. Any one of them is liable to be the big man for any given night."[xxi]

Babe's balanced freshmen squad featured players whose names would fill out the box scores of MSU varsity basketball games for the next three years. Leland Mitchell, a 6' 4" forward from Kiln,

Mississippi, led the freshmen team in scoring with 20.3 points per game average. The versatile and aggressive wing man stayed at the top of the team's offensive charts throughout his varsity career. Joe Dan Gold of Benton, Kentucky, held the other wing spot. Known for his rugged play, the 6' 5" forward emerged at the varsity level as a team leader and would captain the team his senior year. W. D. "Red" Stroud from Forest, Mississippi, keyed the offense. Gold may have been the team leader, but the 6' 1" Stroud was the floor leader with his ball handling and scoring.[xxii]

In the middle for the frosh quintet stood high school standout, Bobby Shows. Lewis Lord, writing for UPI, said, "Several coaches reportedly have been impressed with the talents of 6' 7" Bobby Shows. 'With normal development,' McCarthy says, 'he will be a fine center. He's big and rugged under the basket, a fine rebounder who has hit as high as 31 points. He never misses a free throw.'" Bobby put up 18.3 points per game his freshman year.[xxiii]

Aubrey Nichols grew up near Starkville in little New Hope, Mississippi, and dreamed of playing for State. During his senior year of high school, he followed the freshmen team that Bobby played on at State. "They were a very special group. They didn't just beat you -- they tattooed you! Everybody they played," Nichols said. The next year, he enrolled at State and played for the freshmen team and then played another three years on varsity.

When the varsity Maroons boasted the rising star of Bailey Howell, they enjoyed a season with only one loss and a conference championship. But in 1960 with Howell gone and playing basketball at the professional level, the varsity team Bobby's freshman year was, in Bobby's words, "not very good." Every Friday the freshmen would scrimmage the varsity "and about two out of every three Fridays, we'd take 'em down. So we were pretty good."

Off the court

The classroom for Bobby was more of a work in progress, but a project Bobby would conquer. His high school English teacher told Bobby he would never make it in college. Bobby proved his teacher a false prophet. Through hard work and determination, Bobby made the dean's list his junior and senior years at State.

Bobby said his freshman year was not all that exciting, an apt description of a daily schedule dominated by the routine required of a student athlete. "We played basketball, went to school and ate, that was about all. We did a little studying," Bobby said. He also got involved with the Baptist Student Union (BSU). Bobby grew up in and around church as much as school, so when invited, Bobby didn't hesitate to participate in BSU. But, he said, his participation did not spring from any deep spiritual motivation. For Bobby, BSU offered one of the only respites from the drudgery of classes, practice and life in the athletic dorms. Bobby's BSU involvement would play the central role in his personal spiritual awakening, and eventual vocational choices, but at the time BSU provided a welcome social outlet for a lonely freshman.

Military training through the Reserve Officers Training Corp, or ROTC, was required curriculum for young men on most college campuses. Bobby enrolled but neither he nor ROTC took to one another very well. Size presented a problem for Bobby as he tried to fit into an institution with a strict code of conformity and uniform dress. Bobby did not fit standard issue. Wearing a size 15 shoe and with an inseam of about 37", he had to come up with his own shoes, and army-issue pants were three inches too short.

In a scene straight out of the 1958 Andy Griffith movie "No Time for Sergeants," Bobby learned the hard way he didn't quite measure up to the standards of the cadet officers to whom he reported. Bobby still uses colorful language to describe the student officers who took delight in finding fault.

"These little peep squeaks that come about belly high (would come around and say), 'Mr. [Shoes], you don't have the right shoes and you don't have the right clothes. I'm giving you a demerit for your shoes and a demerit because you don't have the right size of pants on.' I'd go over to the ROTC office and polish brass and sweep floors and get all my demerits worked off. I would have loved to have cold-cocked a couple of those fellas," he recalled.

Height kept Bobby awash in ROTC demerits but also rescued him from the draft. The military had a height limit of 6'6". Apparently the military considered such height a physical defect. "The draft board had given me a draft number. I had the same draft number as Mohammad Ali, which was for the mental or physically defective. You can decide which one of those fit me," Bobby said.

In one of those what if's that mark every life, Bobby turned down scholarship offers his senior year in high school from all three military academies. The recruiter from the air force academy wrote him and said, "By the time we measure you, you will be 6'6." "I don't have the letter but I remember that. And I was 6' 7 ¼" at that time barefoot!" Bobby said.

The basketball team became Bobby's family, his fraternity of brothers. "As freshman we really did things together because of the upperclassmen. That was back when they could do about anything they wanted to a freshman," Bobby said. He described the treatment they received from upperclassmen, including buzz cuts, gauntlet runs, wild-goose chases, body tic-tac-toe, various forms of humiliation. "Every freshman got the haircut and had to wear the beanie," Bobby said. "I still got my beanie. Those were not very nice days."

When Bobby visited his family, his younger brothers always challenged him to a game of hoops. "Bobby made me a better ballplayer," Scotty said. "We'd play a lot of one-on-one stuff, so the only way I could possibly score was to do all kind of crazy things. He'd block everything I'd shoot, so I had to do all kind of – when I say fall away I mean jump and fall – I shot an unconventional hook because he'd even block my hook. So that made me a lot better ballplayer." Scotty, who would eventually play on the freshman basketball team at State, said he and younger brother Glenn never beat their big brother in those one-on-one and two-on-one basketball sessions. "Even as we got older I never beat him one on one," Scotty said. Years later Scotty came to the hospital to visit his brother who had suffered a heart attack. He leaned over and whispered in Bobby's ear, "Now Bobby, at 3 o'clock this afternoon I challenge you to one on one and if you don't show up I am going to win. In theory, I won one game," Scotty said.

Rockmont

Black Mountain, North Carolina, is a town far from Starkville, Mississippi, in western North Carolina's Blue Ridge Mountains near Ashville. Bobby made his way to Black Mountain the summer after his freshman year and four more summers while in college. Standing sentry over the Black Mountain community are the Christian campgrounds of Ridgecrest Conference Center to the east and Rockmont Camp for Boys to the west. Many times Bobby returned to Ridgecrest, one of two national encampments for Southern Baptists. Rockmont, ensconced in the foothills of Pisgah National Forest, shaped Bobby's life and career as much as anything he learned in Starkville, teaching him that athletics and recreation can be tools for ministry.

Rockmont Manager George Pickering founded the camp on the grounds of a defunct college campus and turned it into an elite Christian retreat for boys. Pickering, who formerly managed Ridgecrest Camp for Boys, had many Southern Baptist connections. One of his friends was director of the Baptist Student Union in Starkville. Frank Horton introduced Pickering to Bobby during a summer-staff recruiting swing through the South. For ten weeks, Bobby served as a counselor responsible for ten boys who lived in his cabin. "It was a very rich camp. You had to have money to go," Bobby said.

Ben McKibbens was a big old football player from Laurel, Mississippi, who also spent several summers at Rockmont as a counselor. He started going out to North Carolina each summer when he was only 13 or 14 to attend Camp Ridgecrest. There he met George Pickering who recruited him to be a counselor during summers while at college. When McKibbens and Shows were counselors, it was a big deal to have a staff basketball team and, according to McKibbens, some counselors were recruited because they could play.

Black Mountain was surrounded by camps that brought in college students every summer to serve as staff. McKibbens remembered Rockmont played the staff at Ridgecrest Assembly, Ridgecrest Boys Camp, Montreat Presbyterian Assembly, Blue Ridge YMCA Assembly, and some other camps.

Some players McKibbens remembered playing with him and Bobby included Mississippi State's star guard Red Stroud, who spent a summer at Rockmont. So did teammate Aubrey Nichols. Other big college players that filled out the Rockmont staff basketball team roster included Southeastern Conference players from schools like Georgia and Tulane. "With those guys we could clean the boards pretty good and I just kind a piddled around with that group. They were pretty good. We won every summer every time we played. It was really fun," he said.

Like Bobby, McKibbens' Rockmont experience stayed with him his whole life. Though work took him far afield from the North Carolina mountains, McKibbens now has a seasonal home just outside Black Mountain on the campgrounds of Hollymont Camp for Girls operated by his oldest daughter.

Sophomore year highs and lows

Following on the heels of a great freshman season and a summer working in the Blue Ridge Mountains, Bobby returned to Mississippi State invigorated and ready to prove himself as a sophomore. But Bobby's season took a hit when his knees did not cooperate. "They would swell up on me and I just couldn't perform," he said.

Bobby quickly found himself in unfamiliar and frustrating territory, unable to play at the previous year's level and competing with three others for the starting center role. "I was relegated to the last man on the bench. We had a 13-man squad. That was probably the most traumatic year of my life. I had never ridden the bench. I didn't know what it was. I would play whenever we were 30 points ahead or 30 points behind in the last 30 seconds. That was the kind of playing I got to do."

Aubrey Nichols, who by that time was playing for the freshmen team, said he never noticed that Bobby was struggling. He said a lot of players find the sophomore year moving up to varsity a big step. Nichols admired Bobby's attitude throughout his playing days at State. "I can remember Bobby having a few little minor injuries and things. When he played, he delivered. He wasn't the kind of guy that was going to complain. He was going to go out and play," Nichols said.

At the time, Bobby wanted to blame the guys ahead of him, but his knees prevented him from playing at a competitive level. He remembered the frustration of playing in pain but finished the season without a diagnosis.

Spiritual treasure trickles to the surface through fissures in the suffering soul. Many a spiritual pilgrim started the journey in college days. For Bobby, the start of his pilgrimage could be expressed in evangelical terms – the humble sinner repents, finds forgiveness and salvation.

In the thrall of his sophomore saga, "God pretty well began to talk to me about my relationship with Him," he said. Up to that point in his life, he had little humility. Though he was raised to know better, nonetheless, he had made basketball his god. "It was the thing (that got me) popularity; it had gotten me an education; it was an outlet for me in every form and fashion. In fact," he said with a wink, "some of the girls, I found out later, dated me because I was a basketball player."

Normally social and friendly, Bobby's emotions began to suffer. He became very angry and at times would lash out verbally. He said he acquired "a real bad mouth." Practice became drudgery. After practice, he would go back to his room. After games, he would return to the dorm and literally cry, he was so angry. "I was supposed to be somebody," Bobby said. "I had to blame God. I had to blame the coach. I had to blame, blame, blame."

Looking back on that time, he believes God was trying to get his attention. Or maybe God had been trying all along to get his attention, but only now in the depths of his personal crisis was Bobby willing to listen. Bobby described how God used others to reach him. "Through the BSU, there were some kids who I think realized what was happening to me personally. They began to really develop a relationship with me." At first Bobby resisted. "I remember one boy coming to my dorm one night and just wanted to sit and talk with me. And he started on the religious stuff as if the world had caved in. I wasn't suicidal. I was just embarrassed. And what I had pinned upon to be my stack pole had gone under," he said.

In the spring with basketball season mercifully coming to an end, Bobby was invited to the BSU state retreat at Gulf Shores Baptist Assembly in Pass Christian, Mississippi. Built on the white-sand beaches of the Mississippi Gulf coast and pushed up against the water as its name suggests the retreat center looked more like a resort than a church camp. Delegates, called messengers, to the 2006 Mississippi Baptist Convention voted to close the Assembly, making the unique church camp one more casualty of Hurricane Katrina.[xxiv] Now in ruins, for decades Gulf Shores Assembly had offered one of the most unique church camp experiences anywhere.

The retreat featured recreation and times to socialize. But preaching services and Bible study held center place during the getaway. Bobby was persuaded to go to the retreat. "The only reason they got me to go was there were certain girls that they told me were coming down there and I kinda liked one of 'em," he said.

While sitting in the meetings, Bobby began to listen in a way he had not listened before. The speaker's topic was pretty pedestrian for Baptist pulpits but Bobby heard the message as if for the first time. "The guy who was speaking was talking about the Lord living inside of your life and that it was more than salvation, it was the lordship and so forth. And it tugged on my heart strings," Bobby recalled.

What Bobby heard was different from his own personal understanding of Christianity. "At that time it was pretty simple: If I lived two days good and one bad, I'm ahead by one day. So it had a lot to do with works. That was the way I thought of it. So at the end of the day I would count up how many good things I did and how many bad things I did and I tried to make it more good days than bad days," he said. But that was not what that preacher was saying. "He talked more about what Jesus could do for Bobby, not what Bobby could do for God, and I realized what I was doing was not cutting it."

One morning early in the retreat weekend, Bobby made his way down to the beach where he could walk and talk with God. With the sand beneath his feet and the sound of the surf washing ashore, he started talking to God. Bobby said he told God, "I got something to say because I can't keep going like this." Bobby said he and God wrestled that night and he has not been the same since.

In the Bible is the story of Jacob the Patriarch who stayed up all night wrestling with God. The book of Genesis describes his tussle with God so transformed Jacob that he limped away a different man, physically and spiritually. So changed was he that he took the name Israel which means, "he has wrestled with God."

That night Bobby "got saved." He described the feeling of comfort that washed over him as going from "rags to riches, from the worst to the best. That's the change that took place." Bobby remembered saying to God, "Basketball is no longer my god. You are my God. But I'd sure like to play some more."

The Mississippi State Maroons completed the 1960-61 season, Bobby's sophomore year, with an overall record of 19-6 and a conference record of 11-3. That would be good enough to win them a conference championship, the first of three consecutive SEC basketball championships, along with an automatic bid to play in the NCAA tournament. But they never got to play in the tournament that year. The season ended that spring without a chance for a national title because the State of Mississippi did not allow college teams to compete against integrated teams.

Junior year

Inspired by his new-found faith, Bobby climbed out of his sophomore-slump doldrums. School became more interesting as he focused on his social studies major and psychology minor. "My junior and senior years were just more fun than my freshman and sophomore years. And I am sure that is true of a lot of people because the first two are so basic."

Bobby's whole life had new meaning. He returned from another summer at Rockmont ready for his junior season on the basketball team. He really worked out hard that summer, determined to see how God might use playing basketball for His glory. "I mean my whole purpose was changed now. I was no longer playing for myself; my purpose for playing was for the Lord," he said.

Graduation thinned the field of competitors contending for the post position. As soon as practice started, Bobby was elevated to the starting center role. Others began to take notice as Bobby improved.

Coach McCarthy used his big man often enough in the 1961-62 season that Bobby played in all but one game and started most of those games. "I would say out of the 26 games, I probably started 20 of them. And that was my best year, my junior year."

Basketball was fun again. Bobby loved and respected his coach. He enjoyed playing with teammates who shared his respect for the coach and for one another.

Bobby enjoyed the traditions of Mississippi State basketball. Most people recognize "Sweet Georgia Brown" as the Harlem Globetrotters' theme song and warm-up music. The MSU team also played "Sweet Georgia Brown" for pre-game warm-up drills before every home basketball game.

The cowbell was another home-game tradition Bobby remembered. The Maroon faithful would bring cowbells and other noisemakers, and "they'd get to beatin' those things and you couldn't hear yourself think. I mean it would drive other teams batty because we'd go to places and they didn't have that, any kind of noisemakers," Bobby said. Since cowbells were banned from the basketball arena, alumni bring them to Mississippi State football games to this day.

Bobby didn't need a noisemaker. He made his own noise running up and down the court. Teammates nicknamed him "Choo." Jimmy Wise, the team manager at the time, explained, "We had a basketball coach at Mississippi State that believed in running his team and having them in great physical shape. We had a lot of drills we did and a lot of the drills we did were endurance drills. Bobby being a big guy, being a guy probably not as quick as some others, he had to go to great pain I guess to get up and down the floor. He made a sound like a locomotive, like a train coming down the track, and that's how he got the name "Choo" or "Choo Choo."[xxv]

On and off the court, Bobby's quiet moral leadership emerged. Nichols said he and his teammates remember Bobby's Christian leadership. "He was the quiet leader that sort of set the tone." Years later, teammate Don Posey would talk about how Bobby exerted that leadership even in the dorm. Posey remembered an incident in the dorm hallway where Bobby called him out for using a dirty word. "I haven't said a dirty word since then in 45 years," he said.[xxvi]

As demanding as college athletics could be, Bobby continued his activities outside of basketball and kept up with his school work during his junior year. He dedicated the year to the Lord and when opportunities came to share his faith, he took them. His status as a major college basketball player got him invitations to speak at retreats, church services, and youth camps. An undated newspaper article in Bobby's personal files reads:

"Johnny Baker was the featured speaker for Youth Night at Summit Church on March 4. Baker is the newly elected president of the Baptist Student Union at Mississippi State University. Devotional speaker for the fellowship after church was Bobby Shows, vice president of the Mississippi State B.S.U. Rev. Drew Gunnells is pastor of the Summit church."

The Baptist Student Union recognized Bobby's leadership ability. Elected vice president, Bobby worked closely with BSU Director Frank Horton. "He would call me into his office we'd sit down and talk about whatever. It was just great." Bobby benefited from the relationship with Horton. "I really loved and appreciated him," Bobby said, and counted Horton one of his life mentors.

Teammate and roommate Nichols said about Bobby's dedication to BSU, "I can remember that if we ever missed Bobby you didn't have to wonder where he was. He was at the Baptist Student Union counseling and helping people and doing the things that he loved to do."

The 1961-62 Mississippi State basketball team started the season with ten straight wins before running into an inspired Vanderbilt team in Nashville, Tennessee. The Commodores inflicted the Maroons with their only loss that year.

Starting with a five-game home stand, the Maroons beat Southeastern Louisiana on Dec. 2, 96-73, and two nights later toppled Southwestern Louisiana, 88-61. Next, Louisiana Tech fell to the Maroons, 81-58, on Dec. 6. Three days later State gave a drubbing to Delta State, 84-55.

The sprint through December continued with a rout of Louisiana College, 113-70, on Dec. 11 and a 69-57 win over Murray State Dec. 15. Bobby had his best game to that point verses Louisiana College, scoring 12 points and pulling down 16 rebounds.[xxvii]

On Dec. 19, MSU handed Memphis State an 83-71 loss. After a brief Christmas break, the Maroons headed to New Orleans for the annual Sugar Bowl Tournament where they dispatched Maryland, 64-62, on Dec. 29 and LSU, 73-51, on Dec. 30.

With the coming of January 1962, the Maroons embarked on what would be a championship campaign in the Southeastern Conference, starting Jan. 6 with a 51-48 victory in Starkville over the Auburn Tigers. Bobby played in all but the Auburn game. "I never got to play against Auburn, never in all three of my college years," Bobby said. He explained that Auburn ran a thing called the Auburn shuffle. "They were small guys and they were quick and it was a continual motion thing. Coach never told me why but I am sure he didn't think I could stay up with it because their center was the same height I was and we were the two smallest centers in the Southeastern Conference." Bobby's assessment of why he did not play against Auburn applied to other opponents, too. He saw limited action against quicker teams, games in which Coach McCarthy often used a smaller lineup.

On the road the second week in January, the Maroons went 1 – 1 losing to Vanderbilt 86-100 and winning a nail-biter over Georgia Tech, 57-56. The Mississippi State Maroons would not lose another game the rest of the season.

Returning home Jan. 17, the Maroons nipped Alabama, 67-40. Three nights later, State took their game up the road to Oxford, Mississippi, where they beat the Ole Miss Rebels, 61-57.

Taking a two-game respite from conference play, the Maroons continued their dominance over teams from the Pelican State beating Northeast Louisiana, 89-79, at home Jan. 27. Two nights later, the Maroons devastated Delta State 106-76, in West Cleveland, Mississippi.

Bobby put up a double-double against Delta State in a game some said was a coming-out party for Shows.[xxviii] Lee Baker, sports editor for the Jackson *Daily News* described Show's performance as the highlight of the game. In his column, "Baker's Dozen," Baker said the former Mississippi prep star had a good first year, but rode the bench as a sophomore on varsity. Finally, Coach McCarthy has a player in Shows, as a junior, to put "into action when the situation demands plenty of muscle around the backboards. And this weekend could be the time that the big boy – 6-7, 215 pounds – will be the most use for the Saturday night foe, LSU, has a 6-10 center in Tom Conklin and Monday's opponent, Tulane, has 6-9 Jack Ardon."[xxix]

The Maroons started February on the road verses LSU and Tulane followed by two other formidable conference foes, Tennessee and Kentucky. Success in Louisiana continued as the Maroons topped LSU, 87-66, in Baton Rouge on Feb. 3.

LSU Coach Jay McCreary talked about Mississippi State and Bobby in particular after his team's loss. "Bobby Shows made a difference. Playing here instead of at New Orleans, as we did before, we should have had an advantage, but if there was any, Shows and Doug Hutton cancelled it," McCreary said.[xxx]

In New Orleans Feb. 5, the Maroons beat Tulane 70-59. The following week, they made what Robert Fulton of the Jackson *Daily News* called their killing northern swing to Tennessee and Kentucky.[xxxi] Fulton quoted McCarthy as he talked about the importance of the next two games. "This is the biggest trip we've ever taken," McCarthy said, "and we'll be playing the two most important games we have ever played. We've got to have both of them to have a chance at the championship. Of course, we've won championships before but we didn't win them on the road like we'll have to do now."

In Knoxville, Tennessee, on Feb. 10, the Maroons gave the Volunteers a thrashing, winning 91-67. Two days later, the Maroons ventured into Lexington for their showdown with the University of

Kentucky Wildcats. Fulton described the task facing the Maroons: "If the ninth ranked Maroons – already saddled with one defeat – hope to repeat as SEC champions they must beat Adolph Rupp's second ranked Wildcats and they must do it on the Baron's home floor and before 12,000 of Rupp's highly partisan followers."

Since the start of Coach McCarthy's tenure at Mississippi State, a healthy rivalry had developed between Kentucky and MSU. McCarthy had taken the Bulldog basketball program to championship level and proved a formidable foe for the Wildcats and their Hall of Fame Coach Adolph Rupp. The Maroons would steal a victory from the 'Cats 49-44, before heading home to finish out the conference season.

The previous year, someone nailed a funeral wreath with the inscription "Rest In Peace" to the door of the Bulldog locker room after the Wildcats beat the Maroons in Starkville. No one knew for sure how the wreath got there. Some believed a manager from Kentucky or one of their fans was responsible. Others suggested the wreath was an invention of McCarthy's motivational genius.

"We kept that wreath all year long. And the next year when we beat them, we put that on the goal," Bobby said. "All I remember was the police coming and getting us out because ... you don't do that kind of thing in Kentucky. We got peppered with everything imaginable, got spit on, called all things imaginable." Kentucky fans knocked the wreath down from the hoop and tore it to shreds.[xxxii]

The Maroons were hardly helpless victims. At the same game the Wildcats won and the funeral wreath showed up on the locker room door in Starkville the previous year, "One of our rednecks got a skunk and put it under Coach Rupp's seat. And that fired him up 'cause that stunk up that whole building," Bobby recalled.

In that killing swing north, Coach McCarthy employed contrasting strategies with Show's playing more verses Tennessee and less verses Kentucky. Against Kentucky, McCarthy used a slowdown style that the Wildcats struggled to solve, according to Lee Baker. Baker quoted Billy Thompson, of the *Lexington Herald-Leader*, who wrote:

"Mississippi State deserved to win last night's game at Memorial Coliseum. And we're not taking a thing away from Babe McCarthy's charges, but Kentucky Wildcat fans are mighty thankful they don't have to watch that kind of basketball – or alleged basketball – oftener than once every other year.

"Professional basketball isn't a popular sport, but one rule the pros do have which should be inaugurated in collegiate basketball is the 24 – second rule. A team must shoot at the basket 24 seconds after getting the ball or forfeit the ball.

"It's a shame that basketball–hungry fans had to be subjected to that brand of play. Hundreds of fans stood in line for two hours to get tickets – standing-room tickets, at that – and then had to witness a ball-control game.

"Scalpers were selling tickets for $25. Once the fans saw what plan Mississippi State was using, they wouldn't have given 25 cents for the tickets.

"Last night's game attracted 13,500 fans. If the same two teams played at UK again tonight, there wouldn't be 135 fans on hand if they knew a cat-and-mouse game would be offered by the McCarthymen. "Mississippi State had only one way to beat Kentucky and that was ball-control. McCarthy knew it and elected to play that way.

"The McCarthymen won the ball game, but they didn't impress any Kentucky fans – and they certainly didn't win any friends.

"That kind of basketball would kill the game quicker than anything on earth."[xxxiii]

Kentucky may have loathed the way the Maroons played the game, but a win is a win and McCarthy and crew celebrated their victory. Robert Fulton reported the scene after the game as McCarthy's team cut down the nets. McCarthy joined his team's celebration shouting, "This is the greatest. Man, this is the greatest." Later in the dressing room he would eventually quiet his team enough to lead them in a prayer of thanks for their victory.[xxxiv]

To put the significance of the game in perspective, the victory by the Maroons was only the 13th time Kentucky lost at home since 1943. For Bobby, McCarthy's slowdown strategy meant bench time, removing Shows after just a little more than one minute into the game but not before he secured two rebounds and committed one personal foul.[xxxv]

At home to finish the season, the Maroons returned to Starkville solid favorites to defend their conference title. According to a United Press International story in Bobby Shows' personal files, "The 8th ranked Mississippi State Bulldogs were a solid favorite to defend its title and force 3rd-ranked Kentucky to battle it out with the unranked

Auburn Tigers for the league's NCAA playoff berth. With its five remaining games all at home and all against teams beneath its class, Mississippi State (19-1) is now expected to win its third SEC basketball crown in four seasons. But, as in the two previous years, segregation policy is expected to force the Maroons to sit out the national playoffs rather than compete against teams which have Negro players. This means the SEC runner up will take the league's berth and makes the Feb. 26 game between Kentucky (17-2) and Auburn (14-5) at Auburn the most important game on the conference calendar."

Florida came to Starkville Feb. 17. Bobby said he remembered playing Florida's 6' 9" All-American Cliff Luyk. Before the game, Coach McCarthy called a team meeting. He turned to Bobby and said, "Your job is to hold Cliff Luyk to one goal less than his average. And, Bobby, you are to score one goal more than your average." Then he turned to the team and said, "That goes for the rest of you. You hold your guy to one goal below and score one goal more." Then he said, "You guys have had a math course. That is a four-point turnaround (per player) – play that times five – that's a 20-point turnaround." MSU beat Florida 67-45. Bobby pulled down 12 rebounds and just missing a double-double, scoring nine points.[xxxvi]

Against Georgia Feb. 19, the game was delayed five minutes because of clock trouble. Referee John McPherson said to the press table: "This is the first time Babe has started stalling when he was even."[xxxvii] State won 83-74. Bobby had another double-double with 13 rebounds and 10 points.[xxxviii]

The next week MSU beat LSU 58-48 on Feb. 24. Two days later, Tulane lost 62-83 to the Maroons. Bobby played his best varsity game against Tulane with another double-double pulling down 13 rebounds and scoring 14 points.[xxxix]

On March 3 Ole Miss came to Starkville only to lose 58-63 to State and assure the Maroons a share of the conference title. Bobby finished strong in the final game of the regular season, scoring 14 points against the Rebels.[xl]

After three roller-coaster years at State, Bobby finished his junior year with renewed expectations for success. In a starting role with the undefeated freshman team, he averaged more than 18 points per game. But the same success eluded Bobby his sophomore year at the varsity level. At the end of his sophomore season and perhaps the lowest point in his young life, Bobby dedicated himself to Christ determined to come back in the fall with new focus his junior year. The tide turned and Bobby started most games his junior year, showing glimpses of the promise seen in the former prep star. With the ups and downs of the three previous campaigns behind him, Bobby seemed poised for a break-out senior season. He averaged 5.8 points and 6.6 rebounds per game his junior year. His field goal percentage was .330, while his free throw percentage was .705.

As a team Bobby's junior year, the Mississippi State Maroons lost only one game and ended the season ranked No. 4 in the nation. They shared the SEC title with Kentucky and received the automatic bid to the NCAA tournament, having beaten the Wildcats during the season. But the mandate in Mississippi to avoid play with integrated teams kept the Maroons home again in March. SEC co-champion Kentucky made the trip to the NCAA tournament in their place.

The summer before his senior year, Bobby returned to Rockmont. Aubrey Nichols joined the staff that summer, too, and drove the pair to North Carolina for what Nichols said seemed like a brief summer because they had had such a great time. Lifelong friends, Nichols and Bobby forged a special relationship. Nichols said that as the two drove through the streets of Ashville, "I can remember Bobby rolling the window down and dribbling the basketball out of the window of the car on the streets of Ashville as we drove through."

Level Fields of Play

CHAPTER 7

Senior Year

Sometime between his junior and senior years, State decided its mascot would be the Bulldog. Bobby and his fellow seniors on the Bulldog basketball team capped off their career with a trip to play in the post-season NCAA tournament.

Bobby entered his senior year ready for a great final season.

Heading into the 1962-63 season, Coach McCarthy predicted his senior-dominated squad could be the best Mississippi State team ever.[xli] Bobby's role on the team seemed one of the only question marks. After winning a starting role half-way through the previous season, it appeared he would remain a starter, but continue to share time with junior Stan Brinker. Lee Baker of the Jackson *Daily News* said Brinker could be the difference in the season in a reserve role or otherwise, while praising Bobby for his contributions to the Maroon's successful '61-'62 campaign.[xlii]

The Bulldogs started with a flourish, extending their 14-game win streak from the end of the previous season to 19 with five straight victories, most notably over Memphis State, 77-66. Bobby scored seven points and snagged five rebounds for the fifth-ranked Bulldogs against Memphis State before fouling out with 9:16 left in the game.[xliii]

The streak would end at 19 when the Bulldogs dropped a contest verses the Virginia Tech Hokies, 65-82. At that point in the season, Virginia Tech had already knocked off perennial SEC powerhouse Kentucky. With the victory over State, the Tech crew extended their win streak to 39 games. After their fast start boosted by momentum from the previous season, the Hokies faded and ended the 1961-62 season with a .500 record.[xliv]

The Bulldogs rebounded to win their next game verses Christian Brothers of Memphis, 106-71, but turned around and lost to Houston, 76-79, in the Sugar Bowl basketball tournament, Dec. 28, 1962. The game went into overtime when four MSU players fouled out and Houston hit free throws to clinch the win.

"Naturally that hurt, losing Mitchell, Stan Brinker, Joe Gold and Bobby Shows at the end. We were just never in position to play our type game . . . we had to press them most of the way and we're not a pressing ball club . . . that's the reason we lost men on fouls in that overtime," Coach McCarthy said after the game.[xlv]

The third-place game over Xavier of Ohio in the Sugar Bowl tournament went the Bulldog's way with a 75-66 win. Next up, the Dogs gave Delta State a drubbing, winning 106-77. Bobby and Joe Dan Gold posted double-doubles, and Bobby finished the game with only two personal fouls. At Auburn, the Bulldogs ended the Tiger's eight-game win streak by posting a 62-53 victory but Bobby's name would not appear in the box score. In an anomaly in Bobby's career at State, he never played against Auburn in a varsity game in spite of being a regular for most of his varsity career.

After Auburn, MSU met the Alabama Crimson Tide in Tuscaloosa where the Bulldogs took it on the chin, 72-77. Smarting from the loss, the Bulldogs returned to Starkville in Mid-January to take on and beat a feisty Vanderbilt team, 58-53, avenging the previous year's road loss to the Commodores.[xlvi]

Next up, MSU defeated Georgia Tech 81-69 in a home stand that ended Tech's 12-game win streak. Ole Miss fell next to the Bulldogs 78-64 before the Dog's lost a non-conference rematch verses Memphis State, 65-71. The win over Ole Miss put the Bulldogs in sole possession of first place in the Southeastern Conference.[xlvii]

The Bulldogs won their next four contests leading up to the fateful rematch with nemesis Kentucky. In State's victory over Tennessee, the Volunteers tried to borrow from Coach McCarthy's bag of tricks by going into a stall but with no good result. A writer described Bobby' play when he came in with 14 ½ minutes left in the game as contributing to "break a Vol slowdown for an eventual 63-59 win." In games verses Kentucky and others in which the Bulldogs employed the slowdown strategy, Shows sat the bench.[xlviii]

For years Kentucky dominated the SEC. The previous season, Kentucky shared the conference championship with MSU, but did not get the automatic bid because they had lost their meeting with the Bulldogs. However, Kentucky got to represent the conference in the 1962 tournament because of the "unwritten rule" that prevented Mississippi State from playing against integrated teams.

Wildcat fans revered Adolph Rupp. In his 32nd year of coaching
Kentucky the veteran coach had a career winning percentage at the
time of almost 85 percent. By 1963, he had won 20 championships
since the league was organized in 1933. He produced great teams and
great basketball players and was already recognized by several halls of
fame, including being named in 1959 to the Naismith Memorial
Basketball Hall of Fame.[xlix] The name Rupp may have struck fear in the
hearts of many coaches and opposing teams over the years, but it only
seemed to bring out the best in the Mississippi State Bulldogs and their
own charismatic coach.

Bobby remembered the Thursday before the Kentucky game
his senior year and the way his coach inspired the team. "I want you to
in your heart and mind to determine somebody you want to dedicate
this game to – somebody you will commit your playing to – and I am
going to pay for your phone call," Bobby recalled Coach McCarthy
saying.

Bobby called his dad. He said, "Daddy, I'm going to dedicate
this game to you. I'm not going to be able to play much because coach
has already told me that I'm going to get to tip the first part of the
game and get the tip the second part of the game and then I'm coming
out." Bobby said once the game started, sure enough "we got the tip,
scored the first two points and we went into the stall and I came out."

Actually the Babe employed a hybrid strategy to the game that
was more of a hurry-up style featuring the fast break, and then a slow
down once the advantage was gained, at least according to Jackson
Daily News Sports Editor Lee Baker. Baker noted that Coach McCarthy
abandoned a zone defense early in the game, bringing Shows out and
replacing him with Stan Brinker, the stronger man-to-man defender.
The Wildcats started the game with a short line up with no player over
6' 5" and two under 6.' They immediately burned the Bulldogs' zone
with their outside shooting. Now with the man-to-man defense in
place, the Bulldogs clamped down on their opponent and took the
lead, 32-27, with five minutes before the half. That's when Coach
McCarthy decided to slow things down a bit. The teams only scored 11
points between them in the last five minutes going into half-time with
State leading 38-32.

Bobby remembered Rupp losing his cool over McCarthy's
stalling tactics. "We were standing out there because there wasn't any
30-second shot clock. You could stand and dribble a basketball the

entire 20 minutes if you could get by with it. And (Rupp) went berserk. I mean veins sticking out, screaming," Bobby recalled. "Cotton Nash was his All-American from out of Louisiana. I remember he took him out of the ball game and grabbed him by the jersey and shook that kid. I thought: 'Man, I am glad I'm playin' for the coach I'm playin' for.'"

When the two teams returned from the half-time break, State renewed their slowdown tactics. The Cats, however, managed to claw ahead by two on what Baker described as some ugly basketball. At that point, Babe throttled the game up sending his boys surging past the Wildcats for the final victory. The Maroon defense held the Wildcats to only 30 percent shooting, while shooting at a torrid 55 percent from the field themselves giving State its second win over the Wildcats in consecutive years – a first in the history of the schools' rivalry.[1]

Baker, always Shows' fan, indicated that Bobby's role was best suited against teams with tall and big lineups. Bobby's limited versatility compared to some of his teammates seemed to play regularly into the strategy McCarthy employed, leaving Bobby on the bench against smaller opponents.

"Bobby Shows had been a vital figure on the spectacular 1959-60 freshman team at State which swept 21 games without a loss. That outfit provided the hard core of State's 1961 and '62 Southeastern Conference champions and still is doing so for the current club which seems destined to add the '63 SEC title as well.

"Of course, Shows has been overshadowed since those frosh days by his other three senior mates – Joe Dan Gold, W. D. Stroud and Leland Mitchell – who have been regulars all the way, while Bobby bench-warmed behind Jerry Graves as a sophomore and has shared starting duty with Brinker this season and last.

"Nevertheless Bobby has made the difference time and again, coming on when more muscle and height would be needed ...

"Shows – 6-7 and 215 pounds – responds well in such emergencies to take the pressure of an opponent's brute strength off State's comparatively midget-sized (by basketball standards) kids up front."[li]

Long bus rides made winning on the road difficult, especially after an emotional win at home. After beating Kentucky, the Bulldogs headed for the University of Florida in Gainesville, for a showdown with the Gators. Unfortunately for State, the Gators avenged their loss in Starkville the previous year with a 21-point win, beating the Bulldogs 73-52.[lii] The setback would be the last regular season loss for the 17-5 Bulldogs and only their second loss in conference play.

In Athens verses the University of Georgia, the Bulldogs reversed their fortunes, defeating the other Bulldogs, 86-75. State shot more than 56 percent from the field and added 16 free throws in the winning effort. Bobby scored seven points and pulled down five rebounds.[liii]

Now only three teams lay between the Mississippi State Bulldogs and a third straight conference championship. Things seemed to go their way, too. Next up, they dispatched Louisiana State, 99-64, followed by a second victory over Tulane, 78-67. State closed out the conference and regular seasons with a victory over Ole Miss, 75-72, using the stall in the second half to win the game.[liv]

Reflecting on the season, Coach McCarthy recalled the undefeated freshman year of his 1963 senior class and that he had predicted they would lead State to a conference championship before they were done. What he didn't predict was that they would do it three years running. "This crew has been almost a coach's dream," McCarthy said. In their three years on varsity, the foursome of Red Stroud, Leland Mitchell, Joe Dan Gold and Bobby Shows helped Mississippi State compile a record of 76 wins to 12 losses. Along the way, they won two conference championships outright, including their senior year, and shared the title once finishing at the top of the league three straight years. McCarthy spoke with pride at what fine young men his senior class proved to be. "They have been easy to coach while winning all the time, always giving 100 percent cooperation," McCarthy said. "They have a tremendous amount of respect and confidence in each other, too."[lv]

With the regular season behind them, the coach and his players turned their attention toward the possibility of playing in the post-season. Despite their successes, McCarthy's senior quartet had never gotten to prove they were a match for the top teams in the country because of Mississippi's unwritten law against racially-integrated games. Now the Mississippi State Bulldogs were ready to buck that policy if given another chance to go to the tournament. "In the past, serious challenges have spurred them to do their very best. They have always risen to the occasion and met the sternest tests," McCarthy said.[lvi]

After beating Tulane to clinch the conference championship, McCarthy pleaded with his statewide radio show audience to support Bulldog participation in the NCAA post-season tournament. It was a shame his team might end its season without the chance to prove itself on the national stage. "It makes me heart sick to think that these players, who just clinched no worse than a tie for their third straight Southeastern Conference championship, will have to put away their uniforms and not compete in the NCAA tournament . . . . This is all I can say but I think everyone knows how I feel," the coach said.[lvii] The student body, which had supported tournament participation in the two previous seasons, voiced their support of the beleaguered team and coach by rallying in front of President Dean W. Colvard's home immediately following the Tulane game. The very next day the Student Senate passed a unanimous motion that MSU accept the forthcoming tournament invitation, and nearly 2,000 students signed a senate petition.[lviii]

The bid to throw off the shackles of the "unwritten law" was underway and gaining support. The Bulldogs seemed poised to finally get their chance to prove themselves on a national stage.

James O. Preston, Jr.

CHAPTER 8

A Gutsy College President and an Honorable Coach

In 1962, after two consecutive SEC championships and two trips to the NCAA tournament thwarted by segregationist politics, Coach James H. "Babe" McCarthy promised his team he would find a way to go to the tournament if they won the championship one more time. With courageous President Dean W. Colvard, and faithful Athletic Director Wade Walker backing him, McCarthy determined to keep that promise. Their leadership proved the difference as events unfolded in what would become an historic stand that would change the face of the NCAA and sports in America.

Mississippi Governor Ross Barnett, was the central figure in keeping Mississippi State home at NCAA tournament time in 1961 and 1962. Elected in 1960 on a segregationist plank, Barnett was determined to protect the sovereign State of Mississippi from the "evils" of integration. But society was changing. By the time the NCAA invited the Bulldogs to the 1963 tournament, Barnett was still stinging from the backlash of interference with the integration of Ole Miss in the fall of 1962. Barnett's political resolve weakened under the scrutiny of federal authorities and in the face of accreditation sanctions against Mississippi institutions. He would not be a force in restraining the Bulldogs in 1963.[lix]

Instead, Barnett leaned on his appointments to the College Board to act. But the board's authority was not clear. The state legislature originated but never gave legal status to the ban on integrated play. Instead, they used their powers of appropriation to enforce the rule. Until and including 1963, the boards of the state's universities had accepted the unwritten law to save their state funding.[lx]

Frustrated the previous year, his first at State, President Colvard was determined now more than ever that the Bulldogs would play in the national tournament. Several papers cited polls of the Mississippi State student body and of the citizens of the state that suggested surging support for participation. Armed with that evidence, Colvard decided it was time to defy the unwritten rule.

Doug Hutton remembered Colvard broke the news to the team the Monday before the tournament started: "He said, 'Boys, you all have worked hard and you deserve this chance, and I'm going to do everything I can so you can go.' Until he told us that, we never even thought there was a chance we would go. Growing up here, we just never had any contact with black people. And you never even thought about it."[lxi]

Mississippi State's board met in Jackson March 9, 1963. In an open meeting, the first of its kind, the board discussed Colvard's decision. Board members defeated a motion to bar the team from playing by a vote of 8 to 3. After a motion to fire Colvard died for lack of a second, the board approved a motion, 9 to 2, expressing confidence in the president and his decision.[lxii]

Though the board's actions received a backlash from segregationists, many in the Magnolia State were supportive. In the Greenville *Delta Democrat-Times*, Hodding Carter said the board's vote "may have been the first meaningful sign that the decent people of Mississippi are sick of letting the professional haters make all the decisions and control the shots."[lxiii]

Ever the adept politician, Governor Barnett released a statement accepting the legitimacy of the MSU board's decision and his hopes for the team's success.[lxiv]

But politicians with less political savvy and more zealous segregationist convictions remained and fought on to interfere with Colvard's decision. One day before the Maroons' scheduled departure, State Senator Billy Mitts, an MSU alumnus who had been a member of the Bulldog cheer squad, and former State Senator B. W. Lawson filed a temporary injunction with a chancery court in Hinds County against the university board, the president and its head coach, prohibiting them from taking the basketball team out of Mississippi.[lxv]

At 9:30 p.m. on March 13, after a pep rally for the team, an MSU spokesman said the game was still on and the squad would leave as planned the following morning. Hinds County sheriffs arrived in Starkville to serve the injunction around 11:30 p.m. State law required an official from Oktibbeha County in which Starkville was located to accompany the Hinds County officers as they served the papers. Since the Oktibbeha sheriff was ill, Chief Deputy Dot Johnson led the Hinds County contingent around Starkville in search of the president, the coach and other defendants.[lxvi]

Luck and some anonymous help intervened on the Bulldogs behalf at that point. Tipped off, university officials devised a plan to avoid service of the injunction.[lxvii] Colvard's plan centered on the belief that he, the athletic director and the coach were the primary targets and could even be arrested to enforce the injunction's edict, "but that they would not dare touch the members of the basketball squad."[lxviii] So Colvard and John K. Bettersworth, MSU vice president, left Starkville for Birmingham where they checked into a hotel under aliases. Coach James "Babe" McCarthy, Athletic Director Wade Walker, and Assistant Athletic Director Ralph Brown, left for Memphis in a rented car, where they caught a plane for Nashville.[lxix]

Failing to find any of those named in the writ that evening, the Hinds County officials departed Starkville leaving Deputy Johnson to serve the papers. The injunction would not be enforced.

Did Johnson defy orders and aid the MSU plot to avoid the injunction? No one ever implicated Johnson, nor did he ever implicate himself. Chancery court records indicate he searched for the defendants but said they "cannot be found."[lxx]

James O. Preston, Jr.

CHAPTER 9

The Game

Arriving in East Lansing, the MSU Bulldogs stepped off the plane and into history. "I don't think it ever entered our minds that this was a history-making thing. We were just basketball players and we wanted to play against the best," Junior guard Doug Hutton said.[lxxi]

The days leading to March 14, 1963, and the flight from Starkville were filled with the suspense of not knowing if the team would get to play at all. "We didn't know until we got on the plane that we were gonna go. That was a time whenever phone calls were checked. We went to class, went to ball practice and came home. This was the heat of the '60s. And there were some nuts out there. The Ku Klux Klan burned crosses in the president's yard, you know, all kinds of stuff like that all during this time," Bobby recalled.

The next day – March 15, 1963 – they entered Jenison Field House in East Lansing, Michigan, and donned new uniforms for the game against Loyola of Chicago. Under the circumstances, no Bulldog fans, boosters, cheerleaders or bands made the trek to East Lansing. "To my knowledge, the only person we had was a news writer. When we walked out on the court to warm up, Loyola's pep band played our fight song for us. I think that was one of the most emotional times I ever had in basketball," Bobby said.

The emotion the Bulldogs experienced leading up to and in the game itself may have taken its toll. "The way I express it was that we had our game played before we ever got there," Bobby said.

Getting the team and coaches out of Starkville and out of Mississippi and the drama leading up to the decision put a strain on the young men. "We had expended so much energy. Just that back and forth emotional part of it was real draining. At least it was on me," Bobby said, later backing away from suggesting the drama was to blame for the game's outcome. "We were a bunch of kids that whatever coach said, that's what we did. We didn't fuss about it." But at least one other player felt that nerves affected the MSU players. "We played tighter than we should have," Hutton said. State's strategy gave them a 6-0 lead out of the gate, but Loyola whittled away, catching, and then passing MSU to post a 61-51 win.[lxxii]

Bobby remembers the game with ambivalence:

"It was an awesome experience, even though I didn't get to play in that game. I've had several questions in my lifetime but that's one question I never got an answer. I played in the consolation game, I played the entire consolation game but I never played in that one. Coach only played six players in that game at Loyola. But the idea was that we were going to run the score up and go into the stall and we did, we had 'em 10 to nothing. And went into the stall and they caught us and they ended up beatin' us 10 points."

After all the work, all the practices and the games, all the sacrifice – to finally get to the tournament – as a player, it was potentially devastating not to play. Bobby's faith helped him deal with the disappointment. First, he had faith in his coach and his coach's decision. "If he said jump, I said how high? If he said I wasn't starting, there was a reason and I never debated it. Later, that bothered me. I would ask myself 'did I not practice hard enough?' I never was told what was wrong."

Bobby also understood the coach had a responsibility, to match up both strategy and personnel that were best suited to winning any game, something he took with him when he started coaching. Bobby knew before the game that he wouldn't start. Coach McCarthy always let his players know ahead of time – but March 15, 1963, of all the games to be pulled aside and given the news: "You won't be playing tonight."

His faith got Bobby through because, "I had changed my philosophy – I'm playin' for a different purpose, I'm playin' for a different God," Bobby explained. "Daddy was more concerned about it than I was. He couldn't figure out how come I wasn't playin' any more than I was." Yet, Bobby didn't think about it that way. "Out of 27 games I played in 26 of 'em. I was playin' in every game and I was playin' not at the last 30 seconds of the game, either. So I was an integral part of the team and a part of the playing."

Bobby has a news clipping showing him warming up before the game. "You can see a picture of me in my warm-ups. I'd of loved to have been a part of it, but...."

Years later Bobby would recall riding the bench during that historic game in East Lansing and incorporated it into talks and counseling sessions. At the time, he did not consider how it affected him, but as he grew older, he understood it as a real learning experience. "I did some talks that I referred to the fact that I understand about riding the bench, and I understand about not getting to do what you want." Bobby admitted that perhaps his ego had grown large again. "I don't know. Maybe this was God's way of kind of humbling me again."

Aubrey Nichols did not remember that Bobby did not play that day. "I know Bobby never complained about it. Sometimes if you don't get the playing time you expect, you kind of get your head hanging low. But he certainly didn't do that. I can tell you I would have remembered that," Nichols said.

Although part of something that transcended sports, the players did not fully understand all the implications of the events. Bobby believes they are the reason Mississippi State did not have any problems when it integrated. "I think that, yes, we did change the philosophy of not just our school but the philosophy of the whole Southeastern Conference," he said.

Nichols agreed, adding that the first step sometimes is the most difficult. He described the game as possibly the first step in changing some things that needed to be changed. "At that point in our lives the most important thing to us was playing basketball. It really and truly was not a situation that we were fighting for a cause. We simply wanted to go and play basketball and do as well as we could and hopefully win the game. But as you look back and you see the things and the comments and people involved and how they felt about it, it becomes pretty obvious that it was a lot more than just a game," he said.[lxxiii]

The 1963 Mississippi State Bulldog basketball team finished the season with a 22-6 record and a No. 6 national ranking in the Associated Press poll.

James O. Preston, Jr.

CHAPTER 10

Ego is a Strange Thing

Little did Bobby realize when he dedicated himself to the Lord that he would serve God, not as a basketball star, but as a sports missionary. Bobby's fortunate involvement with Baptist Student Union and summer employment with Camp Rockmont prepared him for a life of service through sports and introduced him to his life mate.

Rockmont revisited

There is something about the air around Black Mountain.

Lots of people will make the claim for their little piece of heaven on earth, but Black Mountain, North Carolina can make an enthusiastic and convincing case for being "God's country." Just northeast of the hamlet of Black Mountain lies a more famous Christian retreat. Montreat, within five miles of Black Mountain, Rockmont and Ridgecrest, is one of three national conference centers of the Presbyterian Church USA. Billy Graham has a home there and the Billy Graham Training Center at The Cove is located not far from there, near Ashville.

Bobby's summers in Black Mountain provided more than summer salary and solace – they helped clarify his life's mission. Aubrey Nichols, who served alongside Bobby, believed Rockmont was made for Bobby and Bobby for Rockmont. "(Rockmont) did a lot of things that I think that Bobby enjoyed doing. He was able to be around young people. In my opinion it was just a calling – he was just built and born to deal with young people and to try to help those that needed help and guide those that needed guiding. He was just so right at home at Rockmont and in places like Rockmont," Nichols explained.

Bobby spent five summers there as a counselor, at times in charge of as many as sixty boys. "We would have to take the whole crew and backpack up into the mountains and spend the night. They learned to cook out and build fires and all that good stuff." Franklin Graham, Billy Graham's oldest son, was a camper probably no more than 10 or 11 years old when he once joined Bobby and his fellow campers on a trek into the mountains, Bobby recalled.

Rockmont was built on Lake Eden originally as a family retreat area. Later, the property became Black Mountain College. When the college closed in 1956, Camp Rockmont was founded as a Christian summer camp for boys. Its website says camps are known to be places where stories are developed and shared, whether around a campfire, in the cabin, or on the road traveling home. "This place has been telling a story over the last century, though the voices have changed over the years."

Not all pursuits at Rockmont were part of a "higher calling." Rockmont's assistant director may have had other things in mind than Bobby's calling when he recruited Shows. He was a bit of a sports fanatic, and Rockmont staffers would play basketball games, sometimes twice a week against other camp staffs, including Montreat. Bobby's brother Scotty, who also worked summers, said they used to beat Montreat soundly.

With Montreat close by, the chances were good the Shows would run into the famous evangelist or family members. Scotty recalled meeting one of the Graham clan: "I got to square dance with Rev. Graham's daughter, Ruth Graham Lott."[lxxiv] Bobby got a one-on-one encounter with Rev. Graham, but not on a basketball court. George Pickering, the camp director, arranged for Bobby to visit with Rev. Graham in the camp's hospitality center one day. Bobby said he doesn't remember anything that was said because he was so in awe of Graham.

Bobby admitted he and other counselors did some crazy stuff he would never do again, but that undoubtedly contributed to the stories their campers would repeat over the years. One such story featured "Rat Man," a part-man/part-rat character created in the science labs on the old college campus. According to Bobby, the boys had been acting up so "we decided to have the Rat Man come."

With the campers in bed, the counselors rendezvoused around midnight to put their plan into action. The rodent monster – one of the counselors with a poncho pulled over his head and a flashlight beaming up under his chin to create the chilling effect – ran hollering down the hallway. In the bedlam of screaming campers, the "Rat Man" escaped through an open window at the end of the hall.

The other counselors ran into the cabin, firing a 22 rifle into the night after the fleeing villain. Then on cue, one counselor turned the lights on to reveal a blood-splattered scene. Before the lights came up, the counselors splattered catsup around the room while the campers focused on the fleeing Rat Man. By then Pickering had arrived. That little escapade got the offending counselors duty loading and unloading the garbage for the rest of the summer.

Bobby called Pickering a great man and a significant mentor. "He was one of the top positive influences of my life. He was a down-to-earth man who had a great knack for working with kids." Pickering knew everybody by name and he learned enough about each camper that he could place them with other campers and with a counselor who seemed most suited to provide the best experience for each. Bobby learned from Pickering how to use Scripture effectively, frequently quoting from the Bible when counseling.

Jane

BSU Director Frank Horton and Pickering put a "double-team" on Shows to get him to Rockmont. The two mentors innocently set Bobby on an intersecting course with the girl who would become his life mate.

In their heyday, Glorieta Baptist Conference Center in New Mexico and Ridgecrest Baptist Conference Center in Black Mountain, North Carolina, were the crème de la crème of Southern Baptist church camps. Glorieta nestles in the foothills of the Sangre de Cristo Mountains in northeastern New Mexico. The Spanish-influenced architecture and pine-covered hillsides have provided Baptist sojourners a comforting respite as they study the Bible and how to be Southern Baptist Christians. In the summer of 1963, after Bobby was elected BSU president, Horton and Pickering cooperated to allow Bobby to accompany a group from Mississippi all the way out to Glorieta for Student Week.

Bobby roomed with Walter Simmons, the new BSU vice president, so they could get to know one another better. They made a covenant to leave the girls alone that week to focus on the work at hand. The sacrifice for Bobby was all the tougher when he learned that the girl he had dated in spring semester and hadn't seen all summer was on the bus for Glorieta. But he committed to Walter he would not see her – or any other girl for that matter.

One day Bobby and Walter got out of a morning session late and arrived at the large cafeteria to find most of the seats taken. Bobby and his group were ushered to a back area away from where they normally sat. The group of three tables was waited on by a comely gal from Texas named Peggy Jane Terry. Jane was earning her keep in transition from a summer spent as a Texas Baptist Student Union missionary in the Northwest. "I kinda liked what I saw and that was the beginning of the beginning," Bobby said, apparently having forgotten his vow. He and Jane started seeing each other. Bobby met Jane after she got off work to take a walk in the prayer garden, a favorite for young missionaries in love. "I bet we didn't say two sentences to each other. She was quiet and for some reason I was quiet. We saw each other every day and I went back to her table every day," Bobby said.

At the end of the week, Bobby and Jane wrote to one another often – they were both too poor to afford phone calls. Then Jane invited Bobby to come see her over Christmas break. Walter, as it turned out, didn't do any better than Bobby at keeping his vow. Walter met one of Jane's friends at Glorieta, who invited Walter to come to Texas, too. Bobby and Walter left Mississippi in Bobby's 1957 Chevy Belair on Old Highway 80 out of Jackson, driving all the way to Longview, Texas. There they spent Christmas with their girls at their parents' homes. Gas cost 20 cents in Marshall, Texas.

If Bobby wasn't convinced before Christmas, the time spent in Longview settled matters. "We hit it off. Everything was going good," he said. The long-distance romance with Jane continued after Bobby returned to Starkville with letters and the occasional extravagance of a phone call. Walter's romance didn't work out so well, so Bobby headed to Longview by himself during a break in the 1964 spring semester. The two laid out plans to spend the summer working on staff at Rockmont, and then Bobby returned to State, graduating in the spring of 1964 with his master's degree.

In North Carolina that summer, Bobby and Jane got to see one another every day. After work, there was time to take a walk, or sometimes even go into town for a date. One day during each camp session, counselors got an entire day off while campers took over their duties. This arrangement gave staffers a much-needed break while teaching campers leadership skills. Bobby and buddy Ben McKibbens decided to use the day to take their dates to the movies. Afterward, they would go to Table Rock, a prominence in a nearby state park inaccessible except to the most devoted trekkers. With a view hundreds of feet above the valley, Table Rock provided young lovers a great place to get away, enjoy a picnic and the landscape, and to gaze into one another's eyes.

The Book of Judges tells the story of Gideon, one of God's servants and a man called to a seemingly impossible task. Gideon asked God for a sign. In the evening he put out a fleece of a goat or sheep to test God and confirm that he understood what God wanted of him. Bobby had never asked God for such a sign, but the night before his date he put out a proverbial fleece. "God, I don't know the answer to whether I should marry Jane or not but I'd appreciate it if you would let me know today by showing me the most beautiful sunset in the world. If you will show that to me then I will know that I am supposed to marry her. If you don't then I will know I am not supposed to," he asked as he thought of Jane and his plans for their date.

The next morning when he got up, clouds hung low over the mountains. Bobby thought he already had his answer. There would be no beautiful sunsets on this overcast day.

So he and Ben set out with their dates to the movies. When they came out of the theater, the sky was still grey, but not bad enough to prevent the picnic. The quartet bought fixings for their trail-side meal and headed for Table Rock.

When they arrived, the couples found a place at the base of the trail up the mountainside for their picnic, deposited their gear, and headed up Table Rock. After a while, Ben and his date went down to start a fire, telling Bobby and Jane to come along when they were ready.

Bobby and Jane sat, looking across a gorgeous valley with the mountains beyond set against the grey horizon. "I sat down on a ledge and I don't know exactly what the emotion was. I had built up this moment in my mind so that I was going to see the beautiful sunset," Bobby explained. Then, it happened. "All of a sudden there was a light, a penetration of light that just worked its way through the clouds. Just a little bitty beam and it was gorgeous! Fantastic! I've never seen one like it before or since then. So I turned to her and asked her, I said you know – I don't know the words I said, but anyway – I asked if she'd marry me."

Jane remembered that moment. Sitting on that ledge scared her a little. "It scared me, really, but he was big and brave and I knew that he could take care of me if I fell," she laughed. "We were sitting there and he was antsy and we were talking, then all of a sudden this ray of light came out and it just changed the whole sky. It was the most beautiful sunset I've ever seen in all my life. And I mean that. This light began shining through the clouds, then it just burst out and it was just gorgeous. And I remember us oohing and ahhing about the sunset, and then he asked me if I would marry him and it was such a shocker. But then it came out and I said 'yes.'"

They sat there soaking in the moment and the moist air. By then stars poked through spaces in the clouds. As they stood to leave, Jane said, "Before we leave let's sing 'How Great Thou Art.'" The words to the hymn include the verse: "Oh, Lord my God, when I in awesome wonder, consider all the world Thy Hand hath made. I see the stars; I hear the rolling thunder...."[lxxv] Just as they sang about the thunder, "the thing clapped, and I mean it nearly blew me off the mountain for that to happen at that moment," Jane said.

Bobby and Jane sang one more hymn, "Until Then," together on the mountaintop before going down to join their friends. On the way back to Camp Rockmont, they stopped at a public telephone booth and called Jane's parents so that Bobby could ask for her father's permission. Then they called his folks. His father answered the phone. "'Daddy, are you sittin' down?' He said, 'Yeah, what's wrong son?' I said, 'I'm going to get married.' 'Okay. Here's your momma.' That's all he ever said, 'Okay. Here's your momma.' No big deal to him!" Bobby said.

McKibbens remembers that day. He didn't know Bobby was planning on popping the question, but he did notice they were getting pretty cozy. "They were snuggling up over there pretty close for quite a while. As it turned out, he gave her an engagement ring up there that night and it was made out of tin foil from a gum wrapper. After all, we were all pretty short on cash in those days," McKibbens said.

In less than a year, they were married. Jane had signed a contract to teach in Arlington, Texas, and Bobby had already signed to teach and coach in Louisville, Mississippi. So they set the date for June the following year. Robert "Bobby" Shows married Peggy Jane Terry on June 11, 1965, in Longview, Texas.

Bobby visits Jane in Longview, Texas at Easter, 1964.

James O. Preston, Jr.

CHAPTER 11

After the Game of Change, Everything Changes

Mississippi State won and so did the State of Mississippi as State integrated without major incident.

 F inish with a win.

Almost forgotten in the mist of time, Mississippi State closed the 1962-63 season with a win, beating Bowling Green, 65-60, on March 16, in the Mid-East Regional consolation game. Bobby had 5 points and 7 rebounds against the 6' 11 ½" future NBA great Nate Thurmond, who still scored 19 points and pulled down 31 rebounds in the loss.

Upon the Bulldogs' return to Starkville, it was as if the rancorous events leading up to their departure for East Lansing just a few days earlier were forgotten. No armed police force waited to take them into custody. No angry mobs cloaked in hoods and wielding torches or burning crosses awaited them. No university official resigned under duress and no sanctions came down from the capital to censure MSU in any way, shape, or form. In an interview years later, Bulldog forward Leland Mitchell recalled that it was "a positive situation as opposed to what happened at Ol' Miss the year before." [lxxvi]

The lack of a response was no surprise to Starkville. The community never opposed the team's participation in the tournament. Aubrey Nichols looked back on the experience years later and acknowledged that, if anything, playing the game helped bring about change "not only at Mississippi State, but throughout the South." [lxxvii] "We weren't fixed with the notion that we were going to be crusaders. We didn't intend to be crusaders, but as you look back some of the things that you do tend to move you in that direction and I think that's sort of where we were with that basketball game. We're glad that we played it for a lot of reasons a lot of good reasons now and a lot of reasons that we didn't realize at the time." Nichols said. [lxxviii]

It would be another two years before a black student, Richard Holmes, would successfully enroll at Mississippi State University. And his matriculation would occur without rancor, opening the way for others to follow.[lxxix] In 2011, Mississippi State enrollment topped 20,000 with 20.7 percent African-American students.[lxxx]

Starkville resident Douglas Conner said the team's actions in 1963 had a positive effect. Conner, the second black physician to practice in Starkville and a leader in the local civil rights movement, remembered the difficulty white people, who wanted change, faced to speak out in those days. "Any white person who spoke out was … ostracized, but some of them didn't care," he reflected in a 1996 interview. Conner described how much the black and white communities have since come together. When it comes to the Mississippi State Bulldogs, "It's not 'my team' or 'your team.' It's our team,'" he said.

The NCAA refers to the 1963 game between the Chicago Loyola Ramblers and Mississippi State Bulldogs as the "Game of Change," citing its impact on the integration of college athletics. In an interview with ESPN correspondent Dana O'Neil, Jerry Harkness, the captain of the 1963 Loyola Ramblers and one of four African-American starters on the squad, said, "That game, if you ask me, was key. I felt like it was the beginning of things turning around in college basketball. I truly believe that. I just don't know how many other people know about it."[lxxxi]

If the significance of the game played March 15, 1963, was barely understood by the young Mississippians who played in it, they could hardly be blamed. "We just put on our tennis shoes and went to go play," Bobby said. "I don't think anyone was aware of what it meant at the time. We just wanted to go play."[lxxxii]

Recently Bobby's son, Doug Shows, reflected on the significance of his father's team facing down the opposition and playing the game. "I know that my dad's character would have certainly wanted to do the right thing – and the right thing was to play that game and, going forward, to play games regardless of race," Doug said. "I am proud that my dad was a part of that."

As an SEC game official, Doug knows something about pressure situations. He admired how his father's team faced the highly-charged circumstances surrounding the game. "Back in that time, they had to have been under an enormous amount of pressure – something we don't know about today – because of all the things that were going on at the time. But for them to do that and to make a statement, that's something I am very proud to say 'Hey, that was my dad.'"

At least one Loyola player seemed to understand. As if to say "thank you for making the journey," Les "Big Game" Hunter, the Ramblers' African-American star, shook the hand of every Mississippi State player as the Bulldogs left the court following their ten-point loss to Loyola.[lxxxiii]

Finish with a win.

James O. Preston, Jr.

CHAPTER 12

Coach, Family, Minister, Mentor

Bobby left State with two degrees and a fiancée. He began as a teacher and coach, and soon after marrying, found himself in the ministry, working on church staffs and eager to help congregations incorporate sports and recreation. Bobby excelled, receiving national recognition in his field of expertise.

Assistant Basketball Coach, Starkville, Mississippi

The life of an assistant coach is not easy.

Most nights outside of practice and coaching his team means wearing out a car seat while driving to remote destinations. Riding dilapidated bleachers night after night in dimly lit gyms in little rural schools at the edge of the pavement, a recruiter might ask:

"Does the kid have one more growth spurt?"

"Can he make the grades needed to play at the next level?"

"Can he learn to go left, or develop a good hook shot, or …?"

Bobby spent his graduate year at State helping coach the freshman team with Joe Dan Gold and with recruiting. Coach McCarthy listed him as both assistant to the freshman team and his own contact man. "I won't hesitate to have Bobby represent me at any school in the country. He's a wonderful kid," the head coach said. In addition to running drills and preparing for games, Bobby spent many nights on the road, scouting teams and potential recruits. Under gym lights in stale auditoriums, Bobby sat night after night surrounded by locals watching ten sets of squeaking sneakers shuffle up and down hardwood courts. Like any good recruiter, Bobby hoped to find the next Bailey Howell or Red Stroud, or maybe even someone like him who would make his grueling trip into the Mississippi night worthwhile.

Bobby loved it – all of it. Most coaches are gym rats at heart. Their adrenaline pumps a little faster from the sights, sounds and smells of a high school gymnasium. The freshman team at State was good that year, sported some good players such as Bobby's younger brother, Scotty, who had turned down a full-ride scholarship from Mississippi Southern to play for the Bulldogs. "It was hard on me and I am sure it was hard on (Bobby). But Bobby was very instrumental in my walk with the Lord in college. He encouraged me; he gave me my first Bible. He gave me a red Bible and said, 'You ought to be hot after Christ.' I never forget it in the front of my Bible. I still got it. He said, 'Don't use excuses for not serving Christ. You may say, 'Well I am weak and I sin,' but that's no excuse. Confess it and get back into the ballgame. Don't sit around and pity-party. Just go on out and be hot on fire for Christ.'"

After his freshman year, Scotty no longer played at State. But like his older brother, Scotty soon got involved in ministry. Later on when coaching, Scotty said Bobby would speak to his athletes and help with youth retreats in little churches, something he and Bobby continued with their younger brother, Glenn, making ministry a family affair.

That year coaching at MSU taught Bobby he could be a coach and helped prepare him for his career as a coach and sports missionary.

High School Basketball Coach, Louisville, Mississippi

Completing his master's degree, Bobby took his coaching and teaching career to Louisville, Mississippi for the 1964-65 school year. He had done his practice teaching at Louisville.

With his fiancée in faraway Arlington, Texas, Bobby focused on his classroom and his basketball team that fall. He also served as assistant girls' track coach. Bud Turner was girls' basketball and girls' track coach when Bobby arrived at Louisville High School. Turner, who had been at the school about ten years, took Bobby under his wing.

Bobby lived in a one-room apartment during his bachelor year in Louisville. It did have a bathroom, but no stove or refrigerator. When he prepared a hot meal, he cooked on a "space heater" or hot plate. Often the meal consisted of pork and beans and "V-eye-ena" sausages, Bobby said. He had one dish, one spoon and one pot. He still has the dish. On one of my visits to their home, Jane pulled out the dish, a bowl almost the size Jethro used for cereal in the 1960s-era Beverly Hillbilly's sit-com. She mused about how she thinks affectionately of Bobby as a bachelor eating all his meals out of that bowl. An ice chest allowed him to keep milk and juice on hand, but his survival was assured by eating lunch in the school cafeteria throughout the week.

Bobby's classroom responsibilities at Louisville included American history and a class called General Science. According to Bobby, General Science was not about test tubes and dissecting frogs. Instead, the required course taught students "how to write a letter, how to do a resumé, how to do a check, how to go for an interview, all that kind of stuff." Bobby also served as advisor to the school's Fellowship of Christian Athletes chapter.

Bobby remembers his basketball teams doing well, winning more than 20 games each year. He taught his players more than basketball. He cared about more than whether a boy could shoot a jump shot. Since his sophomore year at State and his conversion, Bobby remained committed to Christ and to serving, especially through sports. Gradually, as he transitioned from player to coach, Bobby found new ways to serve God, share the gospel and minister to others. While Bobby worked at Louisville, Mantee Baptist Church, a little open-country church outside of Starkville, asked him to be their interim pastor and music director. "That was interesting. I'd offer an invitation with one hand and direct the music with the other hand," Bobby said. The church found itself without a pastor and members remembered Bobby from times he had participated with BSU revival teams. Like many small Baptist churches, Mantee Baptist found a regular source of pastors in the BSU, young men exploring a call to ministry.

Though Bobby thought God wanted him in ministry, he never felt called to be a preacher, something his time at Mantee Church helped confirm. Bobby had so many things going on with coaching, teaching, other extracurricular responsibilities, as well as pastoral duties – he didn't have time to prepare sermons. "I'd done a lot of devotionals so I'd combine those together with some kind of sentence so all the devotionals tied together," he said. It didn't take long before he ran out of devotionals. To fill gaps when he had nothing prepared, Bobby brought some of his ballplayers who could share testimonies about how they came to be Christians. Some of them could sing, too.

The little church didn't seem to care. Members were happy to have their young preacher. Bobby spent his energy investing in the lives of the young people around him. In Louisville, he organized a Saturday youth night that met in a nearby community center. He got different groups in the church to provide food and beverages. Youth night reached a lot of high school kids in the area, he said.

In the mid-1960s, revival meetings that focused on evangelism, or winning converts to Christ, were common in churches and communities across the country, but especially in the South. Churches employed evangelists to come lead such meetings. Some of them became quite well known. Bobby worked with other local church youth leaders and pastors to bring a youth revival to Louisville.

Bob Harrington, known as "The Bourbon Street Evangelist," was one of those evangelists who traveled the revival circuit. Based in New Orleans, Harrington was known for his flamboyant white outfits and stage persona, moving about the platform with a spotlight on him and a band blaring in the background. Bobby played basketball in New Orleans several times during his college career. Maybe Harrington saw Bobby play. Whether or not Harrington knew Shows, the youth revival committee agreed to enlist the big-time evangelist and Harrington accepted. Under a tent near the center of town, Harrington preached the gospel and the young people responded. Bobby impressed Harrington so much that after the revival meeting, Harrington asked Shows to go on the road with him as his "PR man." Though flattered, Bobby declined.

Bobby set a goal that year to make sure every boy on his basketball squad got the chance to "know the Lord." Several players made professions of faith at the big-tent revival. Some were Christians when he arrived, but by the end of Bobby's two years as their coach all of his Louisville basketball team members were Christians, according to Bobby.

Woodland Hills Baptist Church, Jackson, Mississippi

Toward the end of his second year at Louisville, Bobby spoke at a retreat for Woodland Hills Baptist Church from Jackson, Mississippi, at nearby Lake Tiak-O'Khata. When the retreat concluded, the pastor and education minister asked Bobby to consider going into church work. "I kind of laughed about it and told them sports and recreation is my thing," Bobby recalled. "They said, 'That's what this is. We are building a recreational center, and we want somebody to come down here and run it and be the youth director in addition to that.'"

By then Jane and Bobby had married and she had joined him in Louisville. With the offer to go to Jackson before them, the young couple prayed for God's direction. When God answered, Bobby began the transition away from public education into an exciting new arena called church recreation. In June 1966, Bobby joined the staff of Woodland Hills Baptist Church where he would serve for the next two years.

Named for Andrew Jackson, who famously kept the old Southwest safe from English invasion and other enemies as a soldier and later as president, Jackson is the capital city and the largest city in Mississippi.

Woodland Hills Baptist Church was founded in Jackson in 1930. In 1966, the congregation built a small recreation center, with a gym, a weight room, shower and changing room and a craft room. While there, Bobby launched the first of several ministry activities that he would expand upon through the rest of his career. He started a sports day camp for children. It was little more than babysitting with a devotional thrown in for good measure, according to Bobby. Later, he would develop a model featuring instruction in a particular sport and structured play integrated with times for spiritual reflection and challenges.

Every player has a certain amount of basketball in his or her system. Most players don't live long enough to get it all out. As a young man in his mid-20s, Bobby still had a lot of basketball left in him. In Jackson, he played in organized church leagues for the first time. He developed a semi-professional team called Fellowship of Christian Athletes to play other organizations for fundraisers.[lxxxiv] The team played games and shared testimonies about their faith during half-times. Over his career, Bobby expanded the model, taking teams of current and former high school and college basketball players to other countries to play local teams and share the gospel.

Working with Woodland Hills youth put Bobby in a position to touch the lives of many young people. There were some good kids in that group, he said, including several who became foreign missionaries.

Camping and recreation went hand in hand for Bobby, at work and at play. Bobby and Jane's good friends Ben and Lauren McKibbens also lived in Jackson at the time. McKibbens recalled a time the foursome loaded up his car and went camping in the Smokey Mountains. "I guess we just had to go back and get some of those mountains," he said. Winding their way up the picturesque road to Cherokee, the two couples stopped at the Chimneys Campground near Gatlinburg, Tennessee, and set up camp. McKibbens said, "Here we are, I'm 6'4" and he's 6'8," I guess. Jane and Lauren and we were stuffed into one little pup tent. We were trying to go to sleep and all of a sudden a bear stuck his head in the tent. A big black bear!" They shooed the bear away but nobody slept much after that, according to McKibbens.

Bobby entered church recreation at the very beginning of the movement which, he explained, started taking off in the early 1960s. In 1964, Southern Baptists sponsored an annual seminar for church recreation leaders, pulling them in from all over the country, but mostly from the South where Southern Baptists were prominent. Bobby attended the third Recreation Lab, as it eventually was called. He did not miss one for years, and soon became a leader in the movement.

By the time Bobby left Woodland Hills, his vision for ministry through sports and recreation had taken a mature form. But before he left, he did something as an adult that he led many young people to do – he was baptized. Baptists practice believers' baptism, that is, baptism of individuals who have voluntarily confessed faith in Christ based on a personal conversion experience. He had determined that his first baptism was not valid. Though baptized as a child, his true conversion came as a young man in college. "I had been baptized once before. But I came to the realization that if I was going to teach kids that they had to be baptized out of salvation, then I needed to do the same."

So Bobby entered the baptismal waters once again. Baptism in Baptist churches is by emersion, a method that requires the individual to be completely submerged under the water so the entire body is immersed. The typical Baptist church building, even in the 1960s, was equipped with a "baptismal pool" large enough for adults to enter waters waist deep.

Rev. Fuller B. Saunders was Woodland Hills' pastor. According to Bobby, he was a real gentleman and a somewhat nervous type. Bobby remembered Saunders feared he would drop Bobby because of his size. "I wasn't as heavy as I am now but I was still the same height. (Saunders) was about 5'10" and maybe weighed 160 pounds," Bobby said. Saunders' solution: he placed a children's chair in the center of the baptistery. "He sat me down in a little children's chair and turned me over into the tub."

First Baptist Church, Shreveport, Louisiana

In 1968, First Baptist Church of Shreveport, Louisiana, called Bobby as minister of recreation. Shreveport was founded in 1836 where the Texas Trail meets the Red River on its way to what was then the independent Republic of Texas. By 1970, Shreveport was the third largest city in Louisiana and continues to serve as a center for commerce and culture at the confluence of Arkansas, Louisiana and Texas, a region known as the Ark-La-Tex. The shared history and geography of the Ark-La-Tex made Shreveport a familiar, if not welcoming, destination for the Shows family. Jane grew up in East Texas among the pine forests, cotton fields, wetlands, and waterways characteristic of the Ark-La-Tex region.

Bobby was never sure how they found him, but always wondered if First Baptist Church's minister of education at the time, Rev. Henry Love, had had something to do with it. Love was from Mississippi, with his wife from Kentucky. Rev. James Middleton was the pastor of First Baptist Church, a big man standing 6' 3" and a "big" preacher.[lxxxv] "He was in the Herschel Hobbs era – that bunch of old preachers who did the radio program, 'The Baptist Hour,'" Bobby said. One of Middleton's predecessors at First Baptist Church was Rev. Monroe E. Dodd, who served from 1912 to 1950. Dodd led the effort in the mid-1920s to develop the Cooperative Program, a unified offering to fund Southern Baptist work. The major focus of the Cooperative Program is funding missionary work at home and abroad. Today, it channels more than $100 million annually to Southern Baptist ministries around the globe.

Bobby remembered First Baptist Church, Shreveport, as the place he learned about missions firsthand. Hurricane Camille made landfall in August 1969 along the Mississippi Gulf coastline. In total, 259 people were killed and more than $1.4 billion in damages were attributed to the storm. Bobby took several groups of men, as well as youth and other adults, to rebuild churches in Camille's aftermath.

Camping skills and character development are central in the Royal Ambassadors (RAs) program, along with religious instruction and Bible teaching. At Shreveport, Bobby renewed his involvement as a leader in the church program and as the associational RA director, which placed him in a regional leadership role with other Baptist churches.

Bobby added football and track to his sports and recreation vocabulary at Shreveport, starting flag football and track programs. Both sports became part of the annual RA Congress, a statewide event. Bobby saw a lot of good athletes come through the RA and recreational ministry activities he led in Shreveport. He recalls one young man named Mike McCain, who was about 6' 6" and went on to play basketball for Louisiana Tech. He also remembers Clyde Lee, who became a punter for the Baltimore Colts, and Cecil Upshaw who would win awards as a relief pitcher for the Atlanta Braves. Bobby played against Robert Parrish during Parrish's freshman year in 1972 at Centenary College of Louisiana in Shreveport. Parrish enjoyed a long and successful career in the National Basketball Association as center for the Boston Celtics.

Bobby played against Parrish on an independent team he helped put together while in Shreveport that played all the Louisiana colleges. He still had a lot of basketball to get out of his system. His team provided an outlet so effective, he played more games that year than in any other in his life. With responsibilities for the church's recreation center and as a husband and a father – Doug was born soon after they moved to Shreveport – Bobby reached an impasse. Confronted by his shortcomings at home and convicted that he was not fulfilling his commitments to his family and ministry, Bobby encountered the Holy Spirit while attending a recreation conference. According to Bobby, that meeting was the first time he realized the Holy Spirit lived inside him. "I don't know what was going on but something happened down there and it just, like, came on. I mean, I am sure I heard that a thousand times but the realization of it never settled in."

The basis for a Christian understanding of an encounter with the Holy Spirit is found in Acts 1, in which Christ said he would send his Holy Spirit to personally reside with believers. The second chapter describes in dramatic fashion the coming of the Holy Spirit to believers and to the crowd that day, the Jewish festival of Pentecost. For Bobby, the realization of the Holy Spirit's presence helped shape his understanding that God works in a person's life in a real and personal way. It changed the way he worked and his approach to ministry. He also determined to strike a better balance between work and family, something that would remain a challenge throughout his career.

Recreation ministry was taking off in churches everywhere and Bobby received national recognition as a leader. Looking back, Bobby said the attention was a bit of an ego trip. He pointed to his training at Recreation Lab as his "seminary." By his second or third year at Shreveport, he had made a complete transition from a focus on sports to a focus on ministry through sport. Up to that point, "I thought sports was the way you made a name for yourself – that's all I knew how to do you know, and nobody told me any different," he said, at least until participation in Recreation Lab.

While still at Shreveport, Bobby visited Scotty who was holding down two jobs – coaching and doing music and youth for a church in Laurel, Mississippi, and one in South Jones, Mississippi. Scotty remembered when Bobby visited that there was always time for friendly competition. "We were always very competitive. So if I came to coaching stuff, or if he came to see me, we'd play one-on-one, we'd play ping pong, we might run a hundred yards, we might play whatever. We always enjoyed playing against each other [in] various sports and stuff. He always ruled the roost in basketball but when it came to ping pong and tennis and those kind a things, I was always a little bit better than he was and I was a little bit faster than he was so that helped me, you know, he couldn't catch me all the time. He would say that 'you always have to come home for supper.'"

Scotty and his wife saw many young people respond to their ministry in the little community where they served. According to Scotty, Bobby brought talented members of his church, athletes and musicians who shared their testimonies and would sing. Early in 1972, Scotty and his wife made the move to full-time ministry leading recreation programs. He became a leader on par with his older brother in the church recreation field. All three brothers entered the ministry. Scotty spent the majority of his career leading recreation and missions ministries at Bellevue Baptist Church in Cordova, Tennessee. Bellevue's nationally recognized pastor and preacher, Rev. Adrian Rogers, personally persuaded Scotty to join his staff. Glenn serves on the staff of the Mississippi Baptist state convention as a consultant on family and other ministries.

First Baptist Church, Springfield, Missouri

Bobby attended the only year in which Recreation Lab was held at Windermere Baptist Conference Center on the Lake of the Ozarks near Camdenton, Missouri. Grady Nutt served as the worship leader. Nutt, a preacher with a Southern Baptist seminary degree, gained national recognition as a humorist on the national television program "Hee Haw" in the 1970s. "He was the only guy that I ever heard tell God a joke. It was during a prayer and I didn't know whether to laugh or what – he told GOD a joke!" Bobby recalled.

One of the Rec Lab leaders had a family emergency and could not keep an appointment with First Baptist Church in Springfield, Missouri. He asked Bobby if he would take his place on his way back to Shreveport. Bobby agreed, and made quite an impression on those he met. Within three or four weeks, his phone started ringing. Soon after, Bobby was wrestling with a possible move to Springfield. "They wanted to build a building. And I said, 'I'm not interested in building a building.'" Bobby went back to Springfield several times to lay out his philosophy for ministry. "We are not going to build a building. We are going to make the programs demand us to have a building. If it gets big enough that we need one I'll know and you'll know it. And they accepted that," Bobby said.

In October 1972, Bobby and Jane brought Doug and all their earthly possessions north from Shreveport, to Springfield. Winter came early that year. A snowstorm settled over Southwest Missouri closing the Springfield airport, forcing the Shows family to fly into Joplin 90 miles west to the only open airfield. Cynthia was born in January 1973.

Bobby spent the first two years of his almost seven-year tenure in Springfield building the ministry, or as he put it, "God let us grow the ministry." He often uses his experiences at First Baptist to talk about recreational ministry. "Some of the people wanted us to build bowling lanes. I said, 'That's a pretty expensive thing. How are we going to support bowling lanes?'" Bobby proposed they promote a league in a local bowling alley before they built their own lanes. It took some convincing, but the church finally agreed to try Bobby's way. "So we promoted [the leagues] and we had enough to completely fill the bowling alley with one league. [We] did that for a year and a half and kept it full, and I said, 'Okay, this is something we need," Bobby said, so the church built a four-lane bowling alley.

Following the same formula, Bobby started racquetball leagues through Southwest Missouri State University, Springfield. The leagues were so successful, the church built a court. When the building was constructed, it included basketball courts, racquetball courts, and a bowling alley. "We included a conversation pit that was sort of a unique thing. Crafts became a big thing. If a new craft came in, there was somebody in Springfield that could do it. We must have had at times fifteen to twenty craft classes going. We had the largest program in all my ministry," Bobby said.[lxxxvi]

First Baptist was in its heyday with long-tenured pastor, Rev. T. T. Crabtree. Bobby, like most men in the ministry, put in long hours. Jane remembered Dr. Crabtree's wife made a comment one time about husbands working so much. "I think that was a part of the '70s. Both of them were such hard workers and what she said I thought that fits me. She said, 'I feel like I am a widow with a living husband.' At times, I felt that way too."

Many Sundays, Jane interpreted for the deaf. Cynthia remembers sitting with her dad whenever he didn't have to sit on the platform. "He would sit over in front of her," Cynthia said. "No matter how old I was if he was not on the platform, I would never sit with my friends . . . it was always such a treat sitting underneath his arm."

Park Hill Baptist Church, North Little Rock, Arkansas

In 1979, Bobby got a call from an old friend, now pastor of Park Hill Baptist Church in North Little Rock, Arkansas. Rev. Cary Heard and Bobby and their families had gotten to know one another well in Shreveport, when Heard served as an assistant pastor at First Baptist Church. Bobby said, "We got to be real good friends. We'd always said that it would be great to work together again."

Park Hill Baptist Church was growing under Heard's leadership and wanted to build a recreation center. Associate Pastor Jimmie Sheffield had visited Bobby a couple of times and wanted to know if he would be interested in serving at Park Hill. According to Bobby, Jane loved Springfield and did not want to leave. In addition to raising the children, Jane worked in the church's deaf ministry and taught at Southwest Missouri State University. "We'd settled in and Cynthia had been born there and everything was just going so well," Jane said. She reluctantly went with Bobby to North Little Rock to interview.

"They had the interview at a home and Bobby went in and all the deacons and the pastor had some questions, and then it was my turn. I was of the attitude that 'I don't really care, you know. I really don't want to go in the first place.' So they were asking different questions about Bobby, so I said, 'Oh yeah, he is just an alcoholic. … and their eyes got this big and I said, 'Oh I meant a workaholic!'"

"I really didn't want to go, but we prayed about it, in all of our decisions we have prayed about them. Every time we knew we were supposed to move. But yet I was still in the mother-hen mode with my nest and everything and even though I knew we were supposed to move, I cried because I didn't want to go," Jane recalled.

At first Bobby wondered if North Little Rock would accept his recreation ministry philosophy. He liked the idea of starting new programs and building new facilities and that is what Park Hill Baptist Church wanted. Bobby's approach to recreation ministry started with building a program before constructing a building. "We are not going to build a building," Bobby said to Heard. "And Cary said 'Why not?' And I said, 'Because you don't need one right now.' He said, 'Well, we are going to start you in the best place I can find,' which turned out to be an enlarged janitor's closet. That was where I started – just room for a desk and a little chair. We laugh about it. We really started with nothing at that one."

Roberta Wallace served as Bobby's ministry assistant at Park Hill, and confirmed the fact that Bobby literally had an office in a janitor's closet when he started. She shared space in a little office with the assistant to the youth director. Later, she and Bobby worked together to help the church construct an activities building where their offices were relocated.

Wallace was dating a coach when the two of them started attending Park Hill. She was looking for a teacher's post in the area when Bobby approached her about serving as his assistant. He had only been there about a year. Wallace accepted and stayed in that position until she retired thirty years later.

Bobby probably worked too hard, Wallace said, confirming Jane's assertion he spent too much time at work. "I used to kind of get on to him because he wouldn't even go home for lunch. And I would say 'Bobby, you need to go home and spend some time with Jane.' She was a homemaker taking care of the kids. He spent too much time working but he wasn't doing it for selfish reasons," Wallace said.

A typical day for Bobby might start before 7:30 a.m., perhaps training a group of counselors for an upcoming camp. Next, he might take a group across town or some other location for a day camp, or other event that might take up the remainder of the day. While in the office, he always had a league or event to plan, volunteers to recruit and promotions to publish. Nights often meant meetings with committees or overseeing activities. Sometimes he went seven days straight or more without time off depending on the time of year and the schedule. Summers were the busiest time, Wallace explained.

As busy as he was, Bobby never complained no matter how much was on his plate. He loved the work and the people he worked with. "He always made everyone he met feel so good about themselves and they all liked Bobby. He just had that way about him," Wallace said. Heard remembers Bobby never complained about the task he was given at Park Hill. Bobby obviously loved what he was doing and the people, too. "Bobby's a team player, of course, going all the way back to his college basketball days. He's a team player so he jumped right in there and did what needed to be done," Heard said.

Park Hill gave Bobby his first major overseas ministry opportunities. In 1989, he took a men's basketball team to Brazil. He developed a high school Baptist Young Men's basketball tournament that grew so large Bobby had to use three gyms to accommodate all the participants. An All-Star team was selected to tour and play games against local teams that summer in South America. Countries on the tour included Guatemala, Ecuador, Venezuela, Mexico, and Brazil. Bobby started camps for children and youth and recreational activities for all ages at Park Hill. He ran intermural volleyball and basketball leagues through the church and any group in the church could have a team. He said it wasn't as much about the game as what was happening on the sidelines, as he put it, "laughing and carrying on. It was a fun time."

At Park Hill, Bobby expanded the sports ministry to include sports camps. One time he brought in a semi-professional team from Memphis called Spirit Express. "These were guys who played college ball and it was my first time to see this work," Bobby said. The team of six or eight members ran the sports camps, and the church provided their food and lodging. Bobby eventually modeled Sports Crusaders from that experience.

It wasn't long before Bobby moved out of the janitor's closet into a gym built to hold all the new activities. By now, Bobby's philosophy of recreation ministry was fully formed. The large size of his recreation ministry required many volunteers. He adopted a method for training volunteers that he called the "Jesus format." Like Jesus' twelve disciples, Bobby would take twelve to fourteen people to mentor as specialists in crafts, socials, drama, coaching or other areas. Each year he held a retreat for leaders in which they would lay out the program for the following year. "We would evaluate what we did last year, what we are going to try to do this year, and draw up our budget. I had good people, good volunteers sold out on it," he explained. His approach to enlisting volunteers was simple. He chose volunteers already skilled in a sport, or craft, or other activity, and then trained them to do the spiritual part. Bobby organized the camp, class, league, or whatever activity, then, "I put that person in charge with me watching them. And in the third year it was theirs. I did all of them like that, every program," he said.

Before he came to North Little Rock, Bobby's senior adult ministry mostly focused on fun fellowship activities. He began to incorporate opportunities for senior adults to do ministry at Park Hill. He started a Small Maintenance and Repair Team (SMART) of senior adults who volunteered to assist people needing help with home repair and maintenance. Soon Park Hill senior adults were running a quilting program, a pillow corsage group that converted the altar flowers each Sunday into corsages to place on hospital patients' pillows, and a team that repaired and maintained toys and furniture in the nursery.

Cynthia, Bobby's daughter remembers her daddy being busy, but said, "I really didn't lack from attention from him. When I was with him I had his undivided attention. I remember being a teenager and driving to his office and even if he was in the middle of a meeting, or if he was meeting with someone and he saw me, I was his priority. He would stop whatever he was doing and say, 'What's going on?' He was just very attentive and loving toward me."

Like most parents, Bobby made time to be involved in the lives of his children. Doug remembers that his father worked a lot of nights and weekends, and would sometimes have to be gone for a week at a time. "I do know that he made a concerted effort to spend time with my sister and me," Doug said. "We also worked out together. In high school as I was trying to get built up, we had a little gym down in the garage that my dad and I worked out a few times a week together."

Cynthia remembers her dad helped her pick out her instrument for band in the seventh grade. "I wanted to play the drums. Well, daddy was like, 'you don't need to play the drums' and I'm like 'no, I want to play the drums!'" Bobby and Cynthia went up to the school and as Cynthia was looking at all the instruments in the room, Bobby struck up a conversation with the band director. "They are just cutting up and talking and the band director begins telling him about this instrument that he really thinks that I should play. He told him that 'she will be able to go to college and get a full scholarship anywhere she wants to go.' So daddy says, 'Really? College? Scholarship?' Out comes this case that is as ugly as a mud fence like this alligator print – huge case. But I am saying, 'Daddy, I want to play the drums!' And daddy says, 'But this will be great! You'll be able to go to college!'"

When they opened the case, there it was – a bassoon. "So guess what instrument I played for the next two years," Cynthia exclaimed. "And my daddy paid for it because I was awful and he had to listen to a 'dying cow.' The family would just leave whenever I had to practice. So he didn't require me to play in band after eighth grade. And I did not get a scholarship for playing a bassoon."

Like most children, Cynthia had little understanding of who her father was before he became a parent. "One time when I was in high school, we had to dress up as if it was the 50s and I went into my dad's dresser, grabbed a ring and tied it on a long chain and wore it to school and didn't think anything of it," she said. "I came home and my dad saw me with the ring around my neck and he said,

'Uh, where did you get that ring?'

"'Oh daddy, I just had it. I didn't read it. I just thought it was your class ring or something.'

"'No, that's actually a really special ring. I've got other rings you can use. That one's really special. So next time you need to ask me and you can wear any of my other ones.'"

Bobby had never told Cynthia that he had been part of an SEC championship team and played in the NCAA tournament. "I was a junior or senior in high school and had no clue," she said.

Later, when Cynthia spent a year at Mississippi College where everybody knew her daddy, she soon learned what her father never talked about. "People would say, 'You're Bobby Shows daughter?' I didn't know anything about his greatness. People started telling me what all he had done. It really wasn't until '96 when MSU went to the Final Four. I remember watching the Final Four and seeing a thing on the "Game of Change" and my dad being in that and I am like 'what?' are you kidding me? No one ever told me and especially not him. And I am his daughter and he never said anything to me about it."

Doug also recalled his father's humility. "That's another huge character aspect of my dad - he's always been very humble," Doug said. "It's harder for him sometimes to even talk about his glory days in athletics. You just kind of have to pull it out of him. Because he's not going to share it with you – he might share a story but he's not going to sit there and go on and on about it."

Doug knew his father was special and turned down opportunities to do other things over the years. "His attitude was, 'No, I want to do what I am doing here. My mission is here. This is where God wants me.' I think his heart was always with coaching and working with youth and I think he had opportunities to become a coach at several different schools throughout the years as I was growing up. But his heart was in another direction – God led him in a different direction as a younger person. But there is no question in my mind he would have been a very successful coach."

When Doug was a junior in high school and playing football, he sustained a season-ending injury. "I had an injury that kind of redirected my focus on some other things and it just so happened that that's when officiating came along," Doug said. Doug had already done some officiating for children's leagues through YMCA. By that time, Bobby was well established as a referee for junior and senior high basketball games and was responsible for putting together his own officiating crew. He invited Doug to help. "My dad had been officiating high school basketball games for several years and I had the opportunity to go with him on occasion to some games. It kind of segued into us working games together and that really jumpstarted my interest in officiating. So that season I was able to jump in and referee with [my dad] at some junior high and some YMCA games and that is where I got my career started. I was a senior in high school."

Figure 1 - Doug, 18, and Bobby in the fall of 1986.

Bobby served Park Hill Baptist Church from 1979 to 1993. Heard has known Bobby for 40-plus years and has happy memories of working with Bobby. "I like to tell people who are not that familiar with him that he's got a heart as big as his body, you know, he's just a big guy with a big heart." Heard said he admires Bobby's sense of humor and ability to relate to people. According to Heard, the source of Bobby's humor was in his Mississippi roots. He said Bobby was constantly making people laugh and everybody just enjoyed being with him.

Cynthia talked about her father's sense of humor, too. She said he was always very fun around my friends in North Little Rock. "He just related so well to my friends. He was so funny. I remember he dressed up like Rocky Balboa's mother and lip-syncing to the youth department 'Hit Me With Your Best Shot.'"

Bobby was far from just a clown, though. "Bobby is a very smart guy," Heard said. "Bobby was excellent at motivating people, organizing things, equipping people, and supervising people. He's good at bringing people along side of him and equipping them and motivating them and putting them into service, giving them an opportunity to serve. He had a first-class program everywhere he went.

I saw him do it in Shreveport, and I saw him do it at Park Hill and, of course, I saw him do it again through Sports Crusaders," Heard said. "When he left Park Hill, it was like leaving a family," Cynthia said. "When he left in '93, they had titled his reception 'Bobby Shows – A Heart of Gold.'"

State Missionary, Jefferson City, Missouri

In 1993, God began to stir in Bobby's heart that it was time to move again. He had served 14 years in North Little Rock, and now the Southern Baptist Sunday School Board in Nashville, Tennessee, invited him to join its Recreation Department staff. At the same time, a church in Mountain Home, Arkansas, invited him to help them build a recreation program like the one at Park Hill. While he considered both exciting opportunities, he received a third call – this one from the Missouri Baptist Convention in Jefferson City, Missouri.

Baptists had come to Missouri and built churches on the front wave of immigration to the territory. Mostly Southerners, these Baptists planted churches beside their corn and tobacco fields along the Mississippi and Missouri rivers and their tributaries. Some of the oldest churches still bear names of rivers and creeks the earliest white settlers traversed, such as Little Bonne Femme and Fee Fee, Cuivre and Auxvasse.

When Missouri became the 24th state in 1821, Baptists were already organized into groups of churches called associations. By 1834, a statewide association was established as a means for frontier congregations in Missouri to cooperate for ministry, start schools and do missionary work. Driven by loyalty to Christ's universal charge to "go and make disciples," Baptists in Missouri and throughout the young nation, committed themselves to activities that helped spread the gospel and sprout new churches.

Fast forward more than 150 years and the state association had grown to a couple of thousand churches. These churches are still mostly small and rural, and still voluntarily cooperating as a state association or convention. Now they have a centralized staff of "state missionaries" who provide leadership to churches and associations throughout Missouri.

In 1993, as executive director of the Missouri Baptist Convention (MBC), Don Wideman was responsible for employing the "state missionary" staff. Alberta Gilpin, seminary trained and loaded with ministerial gifts, led the missions department. She came up through the ranks of the Missouri Women's Missionary Union (WMU), an auxiliary organization of the Southern Baptist Convention with organic tentacles stretching from local churches all the way to the national convention. Gilpin headed up missions education programs for all ages, as well as other age-group ministries and missions programs.

Bobby's work in Springfield caught Gilpin's attention. "I just remember being so impressed with him, with his commitment to the Lord and his commitment to people," she said. With new openings on her staff, she contacted Bobby to recruit him to the missions team in Missouri. What Gilpin had in mind was a position that would put his skills and experience to maximum use. She needed someone to lead work with senior adults, Royal Ambassadors, and church recreation.

With two other opportunities before him, Bobby told his old friend from Missouri, that he could not give her an answer until he was certain about God's direction. Soon he had his answer. Bobby never felt comfortable with the Sunday School Board's travel requirements for its church recreation associate. Then the Shows visited Mountain Home to consider the invitation to lead their recreation program. Within a week of his visit, however, a major conflict erupted in the church and it seemed clear to Bobby that they were not supposed to go there. Now only the opportunity in Missouri remained.

Bobby called Gilpin and agreed to consider her offer. He flew from Little Rock to St. Louis where he rented a car and drove to Jefferson City to meet with Wideman, Gilpin and other staff members. "I felt good about it but I'd never done consulting work," he said. When his meeting concluded and as he drove back to the St. Louis airport, Bobby became more and more certain God wanted him to come to the Show-Me State. "When I got to St. Louis I called Jane and said 'Pack, we are going.' She was so excited to be coming back to Missouri."

North Little Rock was the place the Shows raised their children. After all the years at Park Hill and of living in the same house in the same community, the move was not easy. But Doug had been out of the house for some time and was in graduate school and Cynthia was in college. Bobby and Jane found themselves at a point in their lives where such a move seemed ideal. "I remember it was a very sad day for us at Park Hill," Heard said. "But I trusted Bobby enough to know that he wasn't leaving because he was unhappy, or because he was burned out, or anything like that. He just felt that was where God wanted him to go." Heard knew what Missouri was getting in Bobby. "We were fortunate enough to get somebody like Bobby. I think he's unique in that field all across the Southern Baptist Convention. I never heard of anybody that could do it as well. Bobby Shows is just very gifted at what God called him to do."

The City of Jefferson, or Jefferson City as it is known, is located on high limestone bluffs over the Missouri River on a northward turn from its generally westward meander through the middle of the state. Across the river about a half-mile from the western bluffs, the land rises again into rolling hills covered with oak and cedar and topography hinting at the Ozark Hills that start a hundred miles south. Holts Summit is the first community east of Jefferson City. The year Bobby and Jane moved to Holts Summit, the Missouri River decided to let loose a five-hundred-year flood.

Bobby visits with MSU All-American Bailey Howell at 2008 NCAA tournament.

CHAPTER 13

Opus to a Career

Bobby founded a ministry that is a culmination of his calling to missions through sports. His mantra of reaching people through the common ground of sports is realized in Sports Crusaders.

"And the Big Dog award goes to...."

Every summer Friday, in a gym somewhere at or near a church, counselors pass out honors from the Sports Crusaders camp week. The top honor is the "Big Dog" award and it goes to the camper who shows the greatest character throughout the week in drills, in small group times, and in-between times.

The faces of the children are wide-eyed with anticipation, waiting to hear whose name will be called. They watch the 18-22-year-old counselors and their every move, not only on this day but every day of camp. They are like rock stars to these youngsters, thrilled by the attention and the chance to spend time with these college students. A frequent ritual at the end of each week is an autograph session in which campers seek out their counselors' signatures.

Now the week is almost over and parents and other family members ring the floor of the gym. They listen as the counselors explain what the campers learned that week. Most already know because it is all their children have talked about.

"We learned how to shoot the basketball today."

"I got to lead everybody in stretching."

"I got big-dog points for leading my group today."

The experience is more than childcare for a summer day. Children will remember their Sports Crusader days and some of them will return as counselors when they get old enough. Counselors will move on after college, but for them, the Sports Crusaders experience is just as transformative. They will go deeper into relationship with Christ from their summer spent traveling from camp-to-camp, and working under whatever conditions they find each week.

The challenges teach the young men and women to depend on prayer and one another. They learn to serve and to lead. Some will become full-time Sports Crusaders, raising their own support so they can devote themselves full-time. Others will become volunteers in their churches, bringing the spirit of Sports Crusaders with them wherever they go – often times leading their new church to host Sports Crusaders camps. Still others will go on to serve on the staff of churches and ministries of their own.

It all started with one man who had a vision for how God might use a basketball player from Mississippi. "A lot of people might look at Bobby as just a basketball player," Ben McKibbens said, emphasizing how much Bobby has accomplished in ministry. "He's an outstanding individual – faithful, spiritual, thoughtful, dependable, caring, very well organized, particularly regarding his excellent management of Sports Crusaders worldwide."

Bobby's son said the secret to his father's success is simple. "My dad loves people – he just loves people," Doug said. "And people recognize the genuineness of my dad and they want to be around him. They surround him. They want to listen to him. They want to hear what he has to say and learn from him. On the flip side, he wants to sit and listen to them and so it's a two-way street."

All Bobby had done to this point in his life seemed preparation for what was about to come. As a consultant for Missouri Baptists, he relied on nearly 30 years of experience serving churches and leading recreation and age-group ministries. From his location in central Missouri, Bobby could access the entire state, helping churches and developing his ministry network. Gilpin talked about Bobby's unique giftedness for ministry. "He always made everybody around him feel like they were the most important person in the world. That's a real gift," she said. "He always had time for people and was passionate about his Lord but also passionate about the Lord's work and how he fit into it, and he always considered it a real privilege to serve."

Perhaps it was from his background as a coach and athlete in a team sport, but Bobby always worked well within a ministry team. "Bobby was probably one of the most supportive team members that I can ever remember," Gilpin said. "He was always very gracious and very eager to work and to help out. He wanted everybody to succeed and he did everything he could to make that happen."

The MBC staff was transitioning into a team approach when Bobby came to Jefferson City. The team Bobby landed in already worked well together. Like the staff at Park Hill in North Little Rock, Bobby's Missouri Baptist team was made up of very talented and collegial people. If someone had an idea, they brought it to the team for consideration.

Bobby had an idea.

Sports evangelism still lay at the heart of Bobby's calling. At that time, Missouri Baptists didn't have a sports evangelism ministry. Rather than being discouraged, Bobby saw his new position as an opportunity to start new things. After all, that is what he had done everywhere he had served.

The time seemed right to try something new. Over the years, Bobby formed a vision for synthesizing recreation, sports camps, and training volunteers into one program, like it had never been done before. His vision was for a sports camp experience through the local church that would be called Sports Crusaders. What he proposed was for the church to be a partner with Sports Crusaders in promoting the camp, enlisting campers, and providing sports equipment and a place to hold the camp. Sports Crusaders would provide counselors to supervise the campers, lead the sports training and the spiritual component. Bobby saw the potential in college students to make Sports Crusaders succeed. He also recognized from his own experiences, that those college students could learn about leadership and service and about their own place in ministry.

Bobby learned from his recreation ministry days to hold week-long sports camps that began on Monday and concluded on Friday. Sports Crusaders would adopt a weekly schedule of camps, with a daily duration typically about three hours, which would allow one group of counselors to operate two camps, one in the morning and one in the afternoon.

Bobby proposed to find his counselors on college campuses and campus ministries around the state. He said he would train them at the beginning of the summer, and send them out to camp locations for an eight-to-ten-week schedule.

With permission from his MBC team, Bobby approached Dave Bennett and Shirley Williams to help fund the program. Bennett served as the Baptist state evangelism director, a post that wielded clout and budget for special projects. Williams headed up the Student Ministries program that included Baptist Student Union work in the state. Both department directors governed budgets capable of funding sound ministry projects. Bobby took his two new friends next door to a Mexican restaurant on High Street and shared his idea. "They bought into it right there on the spot. They said, 'What can we do?' and I said, 'Well, I am going to need some money and college students,'" Bobby recalled.

With seed money from both departments, Bobby set out to enlist his first counselors. His first recruit was Tim Seifres, a graduate assistant at Southwest Baptist University in Bolivar, Missouri. Tim had played sports in college and was preparing for a career as a coach and teacher. Next, Bobby convinced his nephew, Dale Shows, to join the team. Bobby visited Dale, a student at Williams Baptist College in Walnut Grove, Arkansas. Dale brought a friend, a quiet African-American young man named Rod. He listened without saying a word as Bobby explained the Sports Crusaders program to Dale, who said, "Sign me up."

About that time Rod spoke up and asked, "You got an extra place?" So he interviewed Rod right then, asking him who he was and why he was interested. Bobby learned Rod McQuerter was a basketball player who never started a game in high school but had gone to Williams College, earned a scholarship and a starting spot. He still holds scoring records for Williams College today.

When Bobby, Dale, and Rod arrived back on campus, Jason Clark, Dale's roommate, came out to meet them. "He came out and says, 'Dale's been telling me something about a sports camp. Tell me about it.' So we signed him up on the spot," Bobby said.

McQuerter later committed, and when Bobby added John Moon from Northeast Missouri State University in Kirksville (now Truman State University), he had his five-person team.

That summer, the team held nine camps with about 300 campers. Missouri Baptists liked what they saw. The next year Bobby was given a budget and Sports Crusaders was off and running.

Officiating

On most Tuesday nights and Friday nights during basketball season, Bobby donned referee's stripes, officiating games in Mid-Missouri. Some refereed for extra cash. For Bobby, officiating was an extension of his ministry. From his days as a coach, to his work running leagues in churches and the community, Bobby worked with officials, trained officials, and hired officials, so becoming an official was no stretch. For more than thirty years Bobby refereed basketball games at nearly every level of competition.

Doug, Bobby's son, is an SEC referee, having worked his way to the top ranks of college officiating. He counts his father as his primary influence and tries to emulate his example. "One of the biggest things is his temperament and his demeanor," Doug said. "He had a great composure in difficult situations out on the floor in handling coaches and handling players. They respected him. The way he handled those folks was outstanding and very professional. I wanted to be like he was and be a good mediator and facilitator of the game."

Doug remembers those first games when his father invited him to be a part of a crew to work a series of games. "As the new guy I'm just sitting in the back seat absorbing everything throughout the discussions. So they are talking about rules, they are talking about mechanics, and I'm just listening." Doug has learned well but remembers he owes much to his father/mentor. Bobby and Jane see as many of Doug's games as they can on television and in person when the game location will allow.

Doug recalls the pride he felt when Bobby came to watch him officiate his first NCAA tournament game. Since then Bobby has witnessed Doug officiating three Final Four games and one National Championship game. "That meant a lot to me just to have him there," Doug said. After the game, they talked about how far he had come from those early days working junior high games in the middle of nowhere, to being on the floor of a national championship game. Doug described the atmosphere and what it takes to officiate at that level. "Make no mistake. There's a lot of intensity and, of course, we have to concentrate constantly," Doug said. "We call it controlled intensity. Certainly there's a lot of built up excitement about each game and that's what makes it enjoyable, but it's also a profession and that's how we treat it."

Doug acknowledged the debt he owes his father. "It's great to have him a part of my career and to be the spark if you will that started it all." That debt extends to the spiritual as seen in a ritual Doug practices before each game. "I pray for my crew that we would be a strong team out there on the floor, to be the best we can be and to concentrate on the game, and to have good health as well – we don't want to have any injuries," Doug said. "Those are the three or four things I ask for each and every game."

Looking back on his father's officiating career from his own, Doug said his father loved officiating at the high school level. "He was a very good official and I do believe he could have worked major college basketball if he had wanted to, but because of his job and because he wanted to be around his family, he wanted to just strictly work somewhat locally."

Doug remembers working a high school game some years ago with one of his dad's friends. "It was a big rivalry game and I remember the head coach came up to me before the game and goes: 'Was your dad going to work the game?' And I think he was assuming that my dad was coming to work the game. Those coaches were like 'that's great you are here, Doug, but– where's your dad?'"

Sports Crusaders, a faith ministry

In 2001, when Bobby turned 60, he decided God wanted to take Sports Crusaders out from under the Missouri Baptist umbrella and make it an autonomous, faith-based ministry. For two years Bobby wrestled with the decision. After struggling alone with the question, Bobby called his family to join him at a hotel where he shared with them his plan and asked for their support. They prayed together as a family and pledged their support and unequivocal approval.

Next, Bobby took his plan to his employers and co-ministers at the Missouri Baptist Convention. They recognized that God was in the plan and pledged their support. By that time, the ministry had added more camps and new sports, added female counselors, expanded camps to churches beyond Missouri's borders, including overseas. Now with the encouragement of friends and co-workers, and the promise of partial funding from the Baptist convention, Shows launched out.

God would provide a strong church partner in Union Hill Baptist Church. Union Hill has continuously served the community around Holts Summit since 1843 when settlers migrated up the Missouri River almost 20 years before the Civil War. No town existed for years, even though a grandson of the original Holts plotted Holt Summit around a general store as early as 1870.

By 2002, Union Hill was in a growing community with a thriving congregation that had a strong recreational program and facilities – no small thanks to Bobby Shows, who had been a member since 1993. Union Hill adopted Bobby and Sports Crusaders, putting the ministry in the church's budget and, eventually, turning over prime space in the recreation center for the ministry's offices. At that point, Bobby moved out of his home's basement where he toiled during the ministry's first year.

Sports Crusaders began adding staff, beginning with Tricia Alberts who worked her way up from running the office and serving as a ministry associate, particularly to high school girls' sports ministries. In 2012, she was named executive director. In 2003, former summer counselor Becky Uffman became director of camp operations. In 2004, Randy Curless joined the staff, keeping his residence in St. Louis and helping with camps in metropolitan St. Louis. On weekends, Curless hosts a sports and faith radio show broadcast in the St. Louis area. Steve Webb and Corinne Meuth also became staffers. In 2005, Chris Sisk, another former camp counselor, came on board. Sisk helped with public relations, special projects and recruiting. Others who were part of the staff during that time included Erin Allman, Amy Knoll, David Percival and Corey Casey.

Health and retirement

Two things can go wrong with a human heart that can be described in plumbing and electrical terms. Either veins or arteries, the "plumbing," get clogged up, or the "electrical system" falters, disrupting the heartbeat. Bobby was about to learn his heart had both problems.

In March 2002, as Bobby sat watching his son referee an SEC basketball tournament game in Atlanta, Georgia, he felt a tingling sensation run down his arms. The tingle persisted but Bobby ignored the ache and returned home to Holts Summit.

When Bobby got home and told Jane what happened, she immediately insisted he see his doctor, Tom Schneider. One look at Bobby and Schneider set up an appointment with Jefferson City cardiologist Dr. James Tritz, who informed Bobby his heart did not have a regular beat, that his pulse was slow and in a-fibrillation. Bobby admitted that he had begun to slow and was experiencing fatigue and shortness of breath. Tritz put Bobby in the hospital for a stint. "How could this be?" Bobby thought. He started most days with a nicely paced jog over about a three-mile course in his neighborhood. A section of his garage holds a weight bench with bar and plate weights that Bobby pushes around in a regular workout. At 60 years of age, he worked full time, refereed basketball games, and hunted when he got the chance.

For a while things got back to normal, but then the symptoms returned. In June, after Bobby failed a stress test, his doctors inserted a pacemaker. Recovering in the hospital room that evening, he sat on the side of the bed and felt discomfort in his chest. Bobby lay down and said he does not remember much after that point. He stopped breathing and coded blue. Fortunately his heart doctor, Tritz, was in the hospital. Bobby was rushed into the operating room. According to his doctor, Bobby's heart was shocked back to life at least 24 times. "I guess it wasn't my time to go. God was not through with me. I made it. My God, Doctor Tritz, and prayers of my Christian friends pulled me through," Bobby said.

Cynthia remembered that night and seeing the waiting room fill up with people who came to pray and wait with her family. "We just prayed and I believe that God miraculously healed him. If you were to ask Dr. Tritz he would tell you the same thing. There is absolutely no explanation for how he survived."

As the dread of the surgery and the uncertainty of the night in ICU lifted, so did the family's spirits. Bobby gradually began to respond and, over time, learned just how bad his situation had been. Cynthia stayed with Bobby at the hospital through most of the ordeal. She remembered that, after he came to, he wanted to sit up in a chair so he could talk to her about what God wanted him to do and to make a list. "He really believed God had given him a second chance, that he wasn't finished with the common ground ministries. It was phenomenal. He was like a dead man and then – he was just so passionate!"

The stronger Bobby got, the lighter the mood in his hospital room. Tritz, Bobby's heart doctor, is a Kentucky Wildcat fan. Cynthia said he teased back and forth with her daddy as he recovered from his surgery. She remembered Tritz saying, "Bobby, I just want you to know that the only way I could get back at you for all the stress you caused me is, I put blue stints in you instead of maroon ones. I had a choice between blue and maroon ones but I chose blue ones."

A few weeks later, Bobby was doing well and in rehab when another attack occurred and he coded blue again. After that attack, the doctors recommended that Bobby get a pacemaker and defibrillator. Dr. Pierce from Columbia, Missouri did the procedure. After a slow recovery and reduced workload, Bobby made it five years before he needed another

pacemaker and defibrillator. "That defibrillator saved my life in August 2007. I had a blackout while picking butterbeans in my garden. When a 6' 7" man falls, it clears out a pretty good row of beans. I fractured my C-7 vertebra, but other than that, life has been moving along and I am grateful for each day," Bobby said.

Aubrey Nichols, Bobby's friend since their days as teammates at Mississippi State, described Bobby as always upbeat and never a complainer even today. "As I think back, I think it is rather astonishing that I don't remember a single complaint coming out of Bobby Shows. Ever! He was always upbeat. He was always the kind of guy where the glass was half full. And I don't think he's changed any now. I know he's got his health problems. We talk about that periodically. I think he's handling that well. It's a serious problem but he's got his cap on right."

Bobby retired from Sports Crusaders in 2008 but on most days you can find him still helping and encouraging Sports Crusader staff. On weekends when he isn't chasing down the highway to see grandchildren, or watching his son refereeing an SEC basketball game, Bobby teaches Sunday School at Union Hill. Jane retired from teaching in 2003 at the Missouri School for the Deaf in Fulton. She and Bobby spend their time between grandkids, volunteer work and hobbies.

Bobby's son, Doug, is an NCAA basketball referee and vice president at a bank in Rome, Georgia. In 2011, he refereed the NCAA championship game in Houston, Texas. He has a wife, Corinne, and two children, Ashley and John. Cynthia Walker, Bobby's daughter, lives in St. Joseph, Missouri, with her husband, Steve, and their two sons Dalton Cole and Caleb Robert. Cynthia is active in ministry through her church and in her local community.

Bobby described the Sports Crusader ministry as it is today:

"All of the staff raise their own support and use their special sports skills to serve their Lord. Since its inception, the ministry has grown from one team to twelve teams, reaching thousands of children and young adults through more than 1,800 camps in Missouri, as well as Alabama, Arkansas, California, Florida, Illinois, Iowa, Kansas, North Carolina, Oklahoma, Tennessee, and Texas. More than 38,000 children and youth have participated as campers and nearly 4,700 have made professions of faith. The Crusaders have also taken the message to several countries that include Argentina, Australia, Belarus, Canada, Ecuador, and El Salvador. There are now four sports that the Crusaders work through: soccer, cheerleading, basketball, and volleyball. It is more than just a camp ministry. It has become a training ministry, preparing individuals and churches to do sports evangelism from their neighborhoods to overseas. Conferences, seminars, retreats, sports revivals, and other things are part of the ministry. Where it is headed, only God knows. We want to be ready to move at His timing to whatever and wherever."

The Bobby Shows family vacation in Pensacola, Fla. August 4, 2009.

Photo courtesy of "A Studio on Wheels," Pensacola.

Level Fields of Play

AFTERWARD

I first met Bobby Shows in 1994.

He stood a head taller than everybody in line to speak to me after I preached that Sunday morning in early November. In a typical Baptist church, after a search committee has narrowed its search down to one candidate, he is invited to a Sunday morning worship service to preach what is called a "trial" sermon before the congregation. I had come to preach such a sermon and after a brief business meeting, was called to be pastor of Union Hill Baptist Church.

When Bobby got up to me in the line, I already knew who he was. The search committee told me about Bobby and his ministry at the Missouri Baptist Convention, but more importantly to me at the time was his volunteer role in leading the church's recreation and other ministries. Others had shared with me how fortunate I was to have someone of Bobby's reputation in my congregation. Knowledge of his stature as a national leader in sports evangelism and recreation had reached me well before I arrived in Missouri. His first words to me I do not recall, but the sentiment was clear: "I am a team player and you are the leader of this team and I will do whatever I can to help you and the team be successful." His actions over the five years I was his pastor proved him true to his word.

I met Bobby's wife, Jane and soon was introduced to Cynthia Shows, their daughter. Doug Shows, their son, was already living in Georgia. I got acquainted with Doug later when he came to town to visit his parents. Bobby and Jane made the move to Missouri from North Little Rock, while Cynthia was in college. Cynthia transferred to William Jewell College in Liberty, Missouri, to complete her degree and be closer to her parents. Since the Shows' move to Holts Summit, Cynthia got introduced to a young man in the Union Hill congregation whose parents were longtime church members and leaders. Steve Walker was getting ready to graduate from the Air Force Academy in Colorado Springs, Colorado, where he had been a starting linebacker for the cadet football team.

When I arrived as pastor, Cynthia and Steve were already engaged and planning to get married at Union Hill that summer. The Rev. Cary Heard, Cynthia's pastor from North Little Rock was already enlisted to conduct the wedding ceremony. Cynthia and her parents sought my counsel as they planned the wedding and I soon got to know the family very well.

I was already working closely with Bobby in the children's basketball league. Though the church had a history of ministry through sports and recreation, Bobby revived such efforts including the league, soon after he joined the church early in 1993. That league brought children from the community into our church's gym for basketball games on Saturday mornings – easily involving as many as eighty to 100 children from year to year. Families filled the gym each Saturday to watch and cheer the teams. During the years I served, we saw many families come into the church through our basketball league.

In 1999, I left the church to join the Missouri Baptist Foundation staff in Jefferson City about the time Bobby was considering starting his own sports evangelism ministry. He visited with me about it at the time and I was among those who encouraged him to pursue the ministry. Once he made the decision to start what would become known as Sports Crusaders, Bobby invited me to be an incorporator, helping him to establish the legal and policy basis of the ministry. We did not act alone. Others helped – people like Daniel Hale, Jim Reed, Hale Rhea and others.

In 2001, Bobby invited me to serve as team pastor for a group of college athletes Bobby and Sports Crusaders were taking to Los Moches, Mexico. During half time of each game, the team shared their faith in Christ. Between games, we visited schools in the area, demonstrating basketball skills and inviting the students to come to our games. The week spent with Bobby and the team exposed me to the scope of Bobby's ministry. Sports opened opportunities for Sports Crusaders to take the message of Christ beyond sleepy little towns in the Midwest; this ministry had potential to reach beyond our shores to other nations.

Bobby often cites a verse in First Corinthians: "I become all things to all people so by all possible means I might save some" (New International Version). Early in life, Bobby learned that sports offer a level playing field to share his faith with people who otherwise might not pause to listen and to places in the world where he might not otherwise be invited except for the attraction of sports. "Finding common ground through sports" became the theme for Bobby's personal ministry as well as his missionary career.

During the trip to Los Moches, I began to consider the idea of writing down Bobby's story but did not pursue the project then. When Bobby's health took a hit a few years later, a couple of board members, staffers, and I filled in for Bobby while he recovered. The idea that a book about Bobby's life would help a ministry transition when Bobby retired took on greater urgency. Bobby's health remained an issue but he soldiered on for several more years before finally retiring in 2008. By 2011, I finally surrendered to the idea that God might be calling me to write Bobby's story.

When I approached Bobby about the project, he responded in his typical encouraging way and quickly embraced the project. He and I met on several occasions with an audio recorder between us as he shared story after story from his life. He opened up his scrapbooks to provide newspaper clippings, personal letters and photographs.

Jane joined in the conversation, and Bobby shared names of other people who might offer some insight into his life, people like Bobby's brothers Scotty Shows and Glenn Shows, son Doug and daughter Cynthia, former boss Alberta Gilpin and college roommate Aubrey Nichols, old friends from Park Hill Baptist Church Cary Heard and Roberta Wallace, current Sports Crusader director Tricia Alberts and friend from Rockmont Ben McKibbens. Vicki Brown provided editing and advice on the manuscript. To all of these people I owe a debt of gratitude.

Today, Bobby maintains an almost daily involvement with the Sports Crusader ministry as an ambassador and encourager.

ABOUT THE AUTHOR

James Preston lives in Jefferson City, Missouri, with his wife, Rachael. He was a pastor in Missouri, Texas and Arkansas and also worked for Baptist denominational institutions in communications and development. He holds degrees from Truman State University in Kirksville, Mo., and two Baptist seminaries. He works in development for the University of Missouri. He continues a ministry of writing, teaching and consulting.

CHAPTER ONE

[i] Mike Christensen, "Maroons Played NCAA Tourney in Black and White," *Clarion-Ledger* (Jackson, Mississippi), March 30, 1996.
[ii] Henry Goolsby, "Changing the times: Bold Maroons Bucked Authority," *Clarion-Ledger* (Jackson, Mississippi), December 29, 1999.
[iii] Christensen, "Maroons played NCAA tourney in black and white."

CHAPTER TWO

[iv] Muriel H. Wright, "The Naming of the Mississippi River," *Chronicles of Oklahoma,* 6, no. 4, December, 1928, 529. There is a story among the Choctaws, who lived in the Lower Mississippi country before the tribe came to Oklahoma, that they and their kinsmen, the Chickasaws, migrated from a far western country long, long ago. When their leaders, the wise prophets of the two tribes, reached the great river, in the van of the people, they contemplated its broad waters and exclaimed, "Misha sipokni!" Misha in Choctaw means "beyond," with the idea of far beyond; and sipokni means "age," conveying the idea of something ancient. Therefore the words of the Choctaw and the Chickasaw prophets meant in substance, "Here is a river that is beyond all age," or "We have come to the most ancient of rivers."

CHAPTER THREE

[v] David Pilgrim, "Who was Jim Crow?" Jim Crow Museum of Racist Memorabilia web site, (Updated 2012), http://www.ferris.edu/jimcrow/who.htm.
[vi] After "Brown vs. Board of Education" in 1954 opened the way to desegregation of public schools, almost two decades passed before public schools were fully integrated in the United States.
[vii] Russell J. Henderson, "The 1963 Mississippi State University Basketball Controversy and the Repeal of the Unwritten Law:

Something more than the game will be lost." *The Journal of Southern History*, 63, no. 4 (1997): 828.

[viii] Ibid., p. 829.

[ix] Ibid., p. 830.

CHAPTER FOUR

[x] Jim Sellers, "Mississippi's Cage Boosters See Shows As Another Edwards," *Jackson (MS) State Times*, (Undated clip from Bobby Shows' personal files).

[xi] Ron Higgins, "Bailey Howells Mom Absolutely Knew Best," January 20, 2012, http://www.secdigitalnetwork.com/SECNation/SECTraditions/tabid/1073/Article/230610/bailey-howells-mom-absolutely-knew-best.aspx.

[xii] Jimmie McDowell, "Tournament . . . Bread Slicin' Near," *State Times,* (Undated clip from Bobby Shows' personal files).

[xiii] "Panther Center Nominated for All-American," *State Times*, March 22, 1959.

[xiv] Jimmy McDowell, "State Snares Bobby Shows, Six-Seven Ole Brook Star: Babe Happy Over Inking Tall Youth," *State Times*, March 16, 1959.

[xv] Recording artist Marty Robbins released his song "White Sport Coat" in January, 1957.

CHAPTER FIVE

[xvi] "Landmark Game: 1963 Mideast Semifinal Was a Game with No Losers," *Associated Press*, March 28, 2008.

[xvii] "Mississippi mourns death of James 'Babe' McCarthy," *Associated Press*, (Undated clip from Bobby Shows' personal files).

[xviii] Ibid.

CHAPTER SIX

[xix] Tom Weir, "All-White '63 team left behind racism to play." *USA Today*, March 29-31, 1996. Mississippi State University basketball coach Richard Williams talking about his 1996 NCAA-bound team.

[xx] Lewis Lord, "McCarthy Sees Fine Cage Future," *United Press International*. (Undated clip from Bobby Shows' personal files).

[xxi] Ibid.

[xxii] Ibid.

[xxiii] Ibid.

[xxiv] William H. Perkins Jr., "Gulfshore Buyer Agrees to No Gambling," *Baptist Press* (Nashville, Tenn.), December 17, 2007.

[xxv] Jimmy Wise, in a personal video for Bobby's retirement recorded at a reception honoring the participants in the "Game of Change," East Lansing, Michigan, March 2008.

[xxvi] Ibid.

[xxvii] Lee Baker, "Stan Brinker, Bobby Shows Put On Impressive Pivot Displays," *Daily News* (Jackson, Miss.), (Undated clip from Bobby Shows' personal files).

[xxviii] Lee Baker, "Maroons Mangle Delta By 106-76, Hutton Pours Through 21 To Lead State's Attack," *Daily News*, Jan. 30, 1962.

[xxix] Lee Baker, "Bobby Shows Provides Highlight For Maroons Against Deltans," *Daily News*, (Undated clip from Bobby Shows' personal files).

[xxx] Lee Baker, "LSU's Jay McCreary Possesses Profound Respect For State," *Daily News*, February 6, 1962.

[xxxi] Robert Fulton, "Maroon Basketeers Walk SEC Plank On Crucial Trip North," *Daily News*, (Undated clip from Bobby Shows' personal files).

[xxxii] Lee Baker, "McCarthy Picture of Contentment After Maroons Manhandle 'Cats," *Daily News* (Undated clip from Bobby Shows' personal files).

[xxxiii] _____, "State's Slowdown Tactic Vs. Cats Goes Back To Bailey Howell Era," *Daily News* (Undated clip from Bobby Shows' personal files).

[xxxiv] Robert Fulton, ". . . Shatters Invincible Wildcats, 49 to 44, Rupp And Co. Forced To Play Babe's Game," *Daily News* (Undated clip from Bobby Shows' personal files).

[xxxv] Ibid.

[xxxvi] Lee Baker, "State Toys With Gators To Close Grasp On SEC, McCarthymen Only Four Wins To Championship," *Daily News* (Undated clip from Bobby Shows' personal files).

[xxxvii] Robert Fulton, "Maroon Reduce Magic Number to 3 With Win, LSU, Tulane, Ole Miss Stand Between Title," *The Clarion-Ledger* (Jackson, Miss.), February 20, 1962.

[xxxviii] Ibid.

[xxxix] Phil Wallace, "Maroon Express Keeps On Rolling, Tulane Falls Again, State Leads 'Tucky," *Daily News* (Undated clip from Bobby Shows' personal files).

[xl] Bill Lunardini, "Mississippi State Edges Arch-Rival Ole Miss For Share Of SEC Laurels, Come From Behind To Whip Rebels 63-58 Saturday," (Unnamed newspaper clip from Bobby Shows' personal files), March 8, 1962.

CHAPTER SEVEN

[xli] Carl P. Leubsdorf, "Maroons Hit Hardwood: Babe Says Team Could Be 'Best,'" *Associated Press*, (Undated clip from Bobby Shows' personal files).

[xlii] Lee Baker, "Mississippi State Takes Floor in Quest of 3rd Title in Row," *Daily News,* October 16, 1962, "The big – in fact the only – question mark is the center, where 6-foot-7 Bobby Shows will start. Shows came a long way last season, winning the starting post from Stan Brinker after 15 games. The starters, plus Brinker and guard Aubrey Nichols, will do virtually all of the playing for the Maroons...."

[xliii] Robert Fulton, "6,500 See State Win in Coliseum: Bulldogs In 77-66 Triumph in Jackson" *Daily News*, (Undated clip from Bobby Shows' personal files).

[xliv] 1962 Virginia Tech basketball schedule, http://www.hokiesports.com/mbasketball/schedule/1962.

[xlv] George Sweeney, "Auburn, Houston in Cage Final," *New Orleans States-Item*, December 29, 1962.

[xlvi] "Bulldogs Take Vandy 58-53 For SEC Win, Last Minute Thriller Sees State Victory," *Daily News*, January 13, 1963.

[xlvii] Robert Fulton, "State Rips Up Ole Miss 78-64 For 4th SEC Win, Stroud & Mitchell Have Hot Night To Pace Dogs," *Daily News*,

January 20, 1963. Shows had four points and seven rebounds in the winning effort

[xlviii] "Cow Palace Feud Resumes Tonight: Maroons Face Old Test From Blue Grass Cats," *Daily News*, February 11, 1963.

[xlix] *The Wildcat Tip-Off*, official program for the Kentucky vs. Mississippi State basketball game in Lexington, Ky., February 12, 1962.

[l] Lee Baker, "Pre-Game Plans Changed Quickly For State In Heat Of Struggle," *Daily News*, February 13, 1963.

[li] Ibid. It is difficult to tell if Baker was correct to say "Bobby had started this game – his last on the home court – as a sentimental gesture by McCarthy in respect for all that young man has meant to Mississippi State, even though the younger Brinker for the past month has been just about the best basketeer, game in and game out, that Babe possesses." Bobby indicated in his conversation with his daddy before the game that he would start the game and come out early.

[lii] Lee Baker, "Florida 'Gators' Bite Bulldog Cagers 73-52," *Daily News,* February 17, 1963.

[liii] _____, "Maroons of Old" Handle Georgians: State Rebounds Hardily From Gatorland Defeat," *Daily News,* February 19, 1963.

[liv] _____, "State Downs a Tough OM," *Daily News*, (Undated clip from Bobby Shows' personal files).

[lv] Cliff Sessions, "Prediction Really True: But McCarthy Underestimated Ability of His Freshmen In 1960," *United Press International*, on or about March 8, 1963.

[lvi] Ibid.

[lvii] Henderson, "The 1963 Mississippi State University Basketball Controversy and the Repeal of the Unwritten Law," 827-854.

CHAPTER EIGHT

[lviii] Ibid., 832.

[lix] Ibid., 840.

[lx] Ibid., 844.

[lxi] Weir, "All-White '63 team left behind racism to play," *USA Today*, March 29-31, 1996.

[lxii] Henderson, "The 1963 Mississippi State University Basketball Controversy and the Repeal of the Unwritten Law," 845-846.

[lxiii] Ibid., 846.

[lxiv] Ibid., 846

[lxv] Ibid., 846-847.

[lxvi] Ibid., 847.

[lxvii] Ibid.

[lxviii] Ibid, p. 848.

[lxix] Ibid.

[lxx] Ibid., 849. Johnson attested on the back of the chancery summons that "after diligent search and inquiry in my county, the within named defendant[s] D. W Colvard and James McCarthy can not be found."

CHAPTER NINE

[lxxi] Weir, "All-White '63 team left behind racism to play," *USA Today*, March 29-31, 1996.

[lxxii] Ibid.

[lxxiii] Aubrey Nichols, interview, February 21, 2013.

CHAPTER TEN

[lxxiv] Scotty Shows and Glenn Shows, interview, August 9, 2012

[lxxv] Original lyrics by Carl Boberg, translated into English by Stuart K. Hine, "How Great Thou Art," The Stuart Hine Trust (1953).

CHAPTER ELEVEN

[lxxvi] Weir, "All-White '63 team left behind racism to play," *USA Today*, March 29-31, 1996.

[lxxvii] Ibid.

[lxxviii] Nichols, February 21, 2013.

[lxxix] Ibid.

[lxxx] "MSU Surpasses 20,000 with Record Enrollment Milestone," *News Bureau*, Mississippi State University, September 2, 2011, http://www.msstate.edu/web/media/detail.php?id=5337.

[lxxxi] Dana O'Neil, "A Game That Should Not Be Forgotten: Mississippi State and Loyola Meet Saturday for the First Time Since Historic Game," *ESPN*, December 13, 2012. http://espn.go.com/mens-college-basketball/story/_/id/8741183/game-change-mississippi-state-loyola-cannot-forgotten-college-basketball .

[lxxxii] Ibid.

[lxxxiii] Weir, "All-White '63 team left behind racism to play," *USA Today*, March 29-31, 1996.

CHAPTER TWELVE

[lxxxiv] Not to be confused with Fellowship of Christian Athletes (FCA), the interdenominational sports ministry based out of Kansas City, Mo. http://www.fca.org/.

[lxxxv] "Southern Baptists Shy From Issue of Church Racial Integration," *Sarasota (FL) Journal*, May 22, 1964. Middleton and Southern Baptists missed an opportunity to take a stand for integration in the denomination in 1964. As a leader among "Deep South" ministers in what would be a majority of messengers to the Southern Baptist Convention in 1964, Middleton spoke against a measure proposed by the denomination's Christian Life Commission encouraging churches to open their doors to "Negroes." Middleton proposed a substitute policy statement that won adoption in an effort to keep the denomination from splitting over the issue.

[lxxxvi] Bobby Shows, interview, April 26, 2011.